War by Other Means

WAR BY OTHER MEANS

A General in the Trump White House

KEITH KELLOGG

Regnery Publishing
WASHINGTON, D.C.

Regnery® is a registered trademark and its colophon is a trademark of Salem Communications Holding Corporation

Cataloging-in-Publication data on file with the Library of Congress

ISBN 978-1-68451-246-1
eISBN 978-1-68451-250-8

Library of Congress Control Number: 2021943473

Published in the United States by
Regnery Publishing
A Division of Salem Media Group
Washington, D.C.
www.Regnery.com

Manufactured in the United States of America

10 9 8 7 6 5 4 3 2 1

Books are available in quantity for promotional or premium use. For information on discounts and terms, please visit our website: www.Regnery.com.

Success is not final.
Failure is not fatal.
It is the courage to continue that counts.

—Winston Churchill

CONTENTS

Preface

It was 7 February 2019. We had just finished the presidential daily briefing session in the Oval Office with the director of National Intelligence. The sensitive and highly classified topics covered in these briefings included information available to only the most senior decision makers.

The president asked me how things were going, and I stayed behind while the others (including the vice president, the White House chief of staff, the director of National Intelligence, and the director of the Central Intelligence Agency) walked out. The only other person remaining in the room was Pat Cipollone, the White House chief counsel. I told the president I was "living the dream."

He smiled and said, "You realize you've been with me three years: from the New Hampshire primary to two years here in the White House. You've seen it all. You should write a book."

I laughed and replied, "I don't do books," and walked out.

But the president's comment that day gave me pause. There had already been many books written about President Trump, but they never seemed to portray the man I knew: a patriotic man with uncanny political instincts, unfailingly loyal to those he felt were loyal to America first.

Donald J. Trump is a fighter. Maybe it would be more accurate to say he is an unashamed brawler when it comes to defending America and Americans. As a soldier, I never found his blunt, belligerent patriotism offensive, as some did. I am proud to have been part of his team and to have worked for his agenda. I am honored to know his family. I am confident that he and his policies will be vindicated by the judgment of history.

During my four years of White House service, I had the privilege of flying on Air Force One and Air Force Two, Marine One and Marine Two; going to Camp David; meeting with numerous heads of state; and even having a private audience with the pope. I visited every continent, save Antarctica, and every war zone involving American troops in the Middle East. I participated in every major national security decision made during the Trump administration, covering issues from the war in Afghanistan to our response to COVID-19.

I spent 1,461 days in the Trump White House. No one in the national security apparatus, as they call it, was there longer. Driving out of the White House complex on 20 January 2021, I asked myself the question every good soldier does after a hard fight: "Was it worth it?"

This book is my answer.

PART ONE

A SOLDIER'S LIFE

CHAPTER ONE

The Education of a Soldier

I grew up in Long Beach, California, part of an upper-middle-class family. My father was an executive in a family-owned oil-drilling business, and my mom was an active member of the local community. My mom was kind and compassionate, but also energetic, direct, forthright, and a fierce competitor, as anyone who played bridge with her would soon discover.

My dad was the only college graduate on his side of the family, so he ran the business operations for K.L. Kellogg and Sons Drilling, his family's oil-drilling business. It was a stressful job, and part of my belief in "America First" economics comes from watching, as a teenager, Canadian drilling companies outbid American oilmen for lucrative California offshore drilling contracts.

Like our mother, we Kellogg siblings were all very competitive. My older brother Mike graduated from the University of Santa Clara and played professional football for the Denver Broncos. Later, he went to law school and became a superior court judge in California. My sister Kathie was an off-Broadway stage actress and lived in the famous Rehearsal Club in New York City. She eventually earned a PhD in psychology. My younger brother Jeff went to the University of Oregon on a football scholarship and later became a councilman and vice mayor for the city of Long Beach, California.

I attended Long Beach Polytechnic High School, a sports powerhouse, where I played football and ran track. I was the only white sprinter on our league-winning mile relay track team, and our varsity football team was one-third white and two-thirds minority, but it never occurred to me that this was unusual (this was in the early 1960s). We played in fully integrated sports leagues, and we all just assumed sports was a giant meritocracy: the best players, the fastest runners, started.

Politics seeped into family discussions when John F. Kennedy ran for president against Richard Nixon in 1960. One day, riding the bus home from school, someone passed me a leaflet stating that if you voted for Kennedy, a Catholic, you were voting for the pope. As part of a Catholic-Protestant family, I thought this would make for a lively Kellogg family dinner discussion, and it did, because our family dinner discussions needed little excuse to become verbal bar fights.

My goal in high school was to receive a congressional nomination to West Point, and that required a series of competitive exams in English and mathematics that would help guide our congressman, Craig Hosmer, in his choice. I took the exams thinking they were something of a formality. My dad had been a campaign manager for the Republican congressman (and navy veteran and Long Beach Polytechnic alumnus) in the days of true retail politics. In the end, my English scores were very good, my math scores were very average, and the nomination was not mine. I became the "first alternate," and the primary selection went to a high school classmate, Richard Doty, which turned out to be a good thing for both of us. Richard graduated from West Point, became an Army doctor, and retired as a colonel.

I needed a new path into the military and picked the University of Santa Clara, which at the time was a small conservative Jesuit school with a solid Reserve Officers' Training Corps (ROTC) program. There were family connections there too: my older brother was there; and the dean of the political science department, Dr. Barney Kronick, was a family friend, having attended the University of California with my mom, dad, and aunt.

I majored in political science while taking many American history classes. I also played football and learned that not everyone felt the way my family did about race. When we arrived at the beautiful northern California campus, Pat Malley, the head football coach, pulled my parents aside and asked if they minded my being assigned a black roommate, namely, fellow freshman Bobby Miranda. My parents were shocked. The answer was, "Of course not." My mother was insulted that he had asked.

Bobby was a high school All-American running back from Encinal High School in Alameda, California. We instantly became great friends—and remain so today—but he was so well liked that he became the most sought-after roommate in the school, and the administration decided to move him around. I never got to room with him again after our freshman year.

Playing football and pursuing other academic interests pushed me from a spring to a winter graduation date, which turned out to be fortunate. I didn't graduate at the same time as most West Pointers, and I was a designated Distinguished Military Graduate, so I figured I had a better chance of getting a military assignment I wanted. What I wanted was the infantry, and I was stunned when I was informed that I had been assigned as an air defense artillery officer. I walked into the office of our professor of military science, U.S. Army colonel Robert O'Brien, told him of my assignment, and asked how I could transfer to the United States Marine Corps. O'Brien, a World War II glider troops veteran, got the message, and I was soon commissioned as an infantry officer.

On my initial assignment request I volunteered for service in Vietnam. That request put me on an exclusive list, a real live volunteer. It also helped land me an assignment with the 101st Airborne Division, the Screaming Eagles, one of only two active-duty parachute divisions in the army, and one which already had a brigade in Vietnam.

On a sunny Saturday morning in early January, I was helping my dad and older brother in the front yard when the mailman delivered my orders. I opened them up and saw the confirmation that I was going to the 101st Airborne Division at Fort Campbell, Kentucky. I should have looked at the back side of the orders. I proudly showed my mom and dad, but mom did not appreciate the notation on the back side: "Officer is a Vietnam Volunteer." She told me, rather forcefully, as only moms can, that volunteering for a war in a far-off land was not a good idea—especially given that, among other possible opportunities, I had been offered a professional football contract with the Montreal Alouettes in the Canadian Football League. The monthly pay of the Alouettes was four times what I would be paid in the military. But my interest was in a military career—and serving in Vietnam.

■ ■ ■

My first stop, in early February 1967, was Fort Benning, Georgia, for infantry officer basic training. Named after a Confederate general, Benning housed the army's infantry, Ranger and airborne schools, and an officer candidate and basic training school. Home for the next few months was a small on-post Bachelor Officer Quarters (BOQ) room with an adjoining bathroom.

My initial entry into the "real" army (as opposed to ROTC training) was attending the infantry officer's basic course with two hundred other newly commissioned lieutenants. Our classes were held in Infantry Hall. In front of the building was a larger-than-life infantry officer statue holding a rifle in one hand and signaling "forward" with the other; the infantry motto, "Follow Me," was carved into the statue's base. Corridors were lined with infantry officer candidate students standing at attention, doing "knowledge training," memorizing all sorts of essential infantry information, covering everything from field orders to weaponry.

While the focus was on book learning (it was assumed we'd get field training with our home units or at Ranger school) our instruction, for the most part, was similar to that given the officer candidate students, minus the harassment. School was five days a week. Weekends, for me at least, were spent in the gym.

After six months, I graduated from the basic course and began Ranger school. *That* was a shock to the system. All the military services send their best, brightest, and toughest to attend the course. It is meant to test your leadership at the point of mental and physical exhaustion. In our course, all the Ranger tactical training officers who evaluated our performance were combat veterans recently returned from Vietnam.

Students wore no rank, only name tags and U.S. Army tags. We were just "Rangers." I learned that immediately when I reported in to the school's senior noncommissioned officer, saluted, and said, "Sir...." That is as far as I got before I rapidly assumed the push-up position and started knocking out push-ups while he reminded me that he was not a "Sir" and that he worked for a living. That was my welcome to Ranger school.

Before I started Ranger school I had moved into an apartment off-post. My neighbor was Major Barney Gill, who turned out to be the Benning Ranger camp commander. I had just taken my place in a student class formation when Major Gill called out my name and announced that I would be the "student company commander for this phase of Ranger school—or until you screw it up."

Fortunately, I had a senior noncommissioned officer, also a Ranger student, as my student first sergeant and some pretty good student platoon leaders. The training was hard, exceptionally hard. Sleep was at a premium, meals too, which you ate on the go. The mental and physical pace was intense, and some just could not make it. In the first two weeks, before we even made it to the evaluated phase of the course, our class had suffered 50 percent attrition.

To earn the coveted black-and-gold Ranger tab, a Ranger student had to pass a majority of his graded patrols. Everything, and I mean everything, in the course was evaluated.

After almost four weeks at Fort Benning, we were moved by military trucks from the Camp Darby phase of the training to the Mountain phase in Dahlonega, Georgia. These were the days before GPS, which is why when you found a good "compass man," someone who could really navigate, you kept him in that position. We had no night vision devices except our exhausted eyes. On more than one occasion, maneuvering at night, I waited for the person in front of me to move, only to realize I was standing behind a tree.

Normally, moving to a different Ranger camp means a change in the student chain of command, but I was retained as company commander. Because we kept the same chain of command, we became a cohesive unit.

The final phrase of Ranger school was the Florida Ranger Camp at Eglin Air Force Base. Its commander was Major Charlie Beckwith, who later became the founder and first commander of the Army's elite Delta Force. Simply put, he was a hard ass. Beckwith gave us what he considered an orientation. His style of leadership was, shall we say, different. Pugnacious and aggressive, he framed the course as man against man, a pure survival of the fittest competition that would determine who would be awarded a Ranger tab. Then he spoke separately with me as the company commander. I told him my men weren't going to operate that way; we were a team and we would pull each other through. Beckwith glared at me and didn't reply, but needless to say he had already marked me down for special attention.

We slept on the ground in Florida, with poncho liners as blankets. Early the next morning I was awakened by a Ranger instructor in my face asking me what time I thought it was. We had missed the first formation. We immediately assembled and formed as rapidly as possible. That was the end of my tenure as company commander, though Beckwith, in his typical gruff style, later announced that I would serve as first sergeant.

Ranger school was just that—a school focused on leadership and tempered by physical and mental hardship. It was physically punishing, but also full of tutorials. We had an especially interesting class on snakes—how to handle them and how to know how poisonous they were. One of our instructors was struck by a poisonous snake and carried on as if nothing had happened until a helicopter arrived with a medical evacuation team. We were told that if we were ever struck by a poisonous snake, we should be as calm as our instructor had been while waiting for evacuation. Andy Sendry, a Force Recon Marine lance corporal who was my Ranger Buddy during the course, gave me a look that said, "Who are these guys?"

They were Rangers.

In Florida, I no longer led patrols but usually served as a compass man or carried the heaviest support weapon, the M60 machine gun. I was unaware that coming out of Dahlonega I had already successfully passed enough patrols to be awarded the Ranger tab so I was now constantly in support positions. The last event—after thirteen weeks of tough training—was a twelve-mile forced march back to camp. For three months, we had been on a virtual starvation diet. Waiting for us at the end of the march was the largest barbecue you could imagine, but no one could eat much; our stomachs had shrunk. I had lost at least twenty pounds during the Ranger course and looked emaciated when we graduated. But, needless to say, I stood proud and tall when Barney Gill, Benning camp commander, pinned the black-and-gold Ranger tab on my uniform and said, "Great job."

We were the only Ranger class to have no "Darby Award" winner for the top graduate. The award is based on peer assessment, leadership grades, academic ratings, and a unanimous vote by the camp commanders. Major Gill told me that I had been the top candidate, but that Beckwith had voted no.

Next for me was airborne school. After Ranger school, it was a breeze. Physical conditioning was not an issue, but jumping from a perfectly fine airplane at twelve hundred feet was. The first jump wasn't the hardest; it was the second, when you knew a hard landing might be in store.

After the first week, I ended up in the infirmary. My feet were shot from walking through the swamp water at the Florida Ranger Camp. I still had raw blisters. The medics told me to stay off my feet for a week, and I was given a week's leave. I went to Destin, Florida, sat in the sun, and soaked my feet in the ocean. A week later, I came back, restarted week two, and went into the third week, jump week, where I made the five parachute jumps that qualified me for the silver parachutist badge.

Finally, after eight months of schools and training, I was ready to join the 101st Airborne Division. When I reported in to Colonel Larry Mowrey, commander of the division's 3rd Airborne Brigade, he informed me that the entire division was deploying to Vietnam. I was assigned to the 2nd Battalion (Airborne), 506th Infantry, the "Currahees," signing in the same day as the new battalion commander, Lieutenant Colonel David E. Grange, a World War II and Korean combat veteran. Grange, who would eventually retire as a three-star general, was a true professional, a great leader, and a stickler for doing things right. With Grange, I learned what "right" really looked like. The lesson started that first afternoon in battalion headquarters, when Grange came in. I was there with two other second lieutenants. I stood up, but the other two kept their seats. Grange, acting very personable, asked a few friendly questions; then, just before he left the room, he turned suddenly and said, loudly and authoritatively, "The next time a senior officer comes into a room—you stand up as a courtesy!" The two seated lieutenants jumped to attention.

Soon after leaving the small conference room, Grange summoned me and asked what I wanted to do in the battalion. I said I wanted to be the battalion's reconnaissance platoon leader. He didn't respond, which made sense, because that position normally went to the most experienced lieutenant in the battalion. The next day, I discovered he had other plans for me and the two other second lieutenants. He called the three of us into his office and announced that in lieu of other assignments we were going to Jumpmaster school. I was excited but had no idea what I was getting into; I was a lieutenant.

So the following Monday, bright and early, the three of us reported to the 101st Airborne Division Jumpmaster school. We sat at the back of the room and tried not to be noticed. Jumpmaster school is usually reserved for paratroopers with experience, and is a rite of passage: an airborne officer is not allowed to command at company or higher level in a parachute unit unless he or she is Jumpmaster qualified.

The crusty old army chief warrant officer, who ran the school, told us what to expect and then asked how many of us had twenty-five jumps, twenty jumps, and so on down the line. He looked at us in the back, and said, "How many jumps do you have?"

"Five."

"Five?"

A silence came over the room. He left for a moment, as if to check why we were there, but he didn't kick us out. We remained in the class.

The three-week course was demanding. We did a parachute jump almost every day. We learned how to pack and rig equipment and deliver "door bundles" so a "stick" of troopers would have equipment, beyond what they carried, on the drop zone with them. Paratrooper safety was paramount. To graduate, a student had to pass a written test, the notoriously difficult Jumpmaster Personnel Inspection (a timed test to identify any parachute or rigging deficiency of three rigged students), and an "actions in the aircraft" test, where the student simulates the actions of a real jumpmaster in flight evaluated by a "Blackhat." Blackhats are airborne instructors who are the demigods of parachute training. In the 101st, they were exceptionally experienced, were all generally twice my age and, to them, a second lieutenant was something to be barely tolerated. The evaluated actions in the aircraft covered everything from how well you observed and identified drop zones, to your safety inspections, jump commands, and confidence.

We three lieutenants passed the written test and the Jumpmaster Personnel Inspection test, but on graduation day, the warrant officer informed us that we had all failed the actions in the aircraft test and therefore failed the course. We returned to battalion headquarters and told Grange what had happened. He showed no emotion, but said, "What are you all doing next week?" None of us said a word. He filled the silence: "You are going back to Jumpmaster school." As Yogi Berra once said, it was déjà vu all over again.

This time we sat in the front row and proudly raised our hands when he asked how many jumps each of us had (fifteen). The course went fine (though on one night jump, I landed almost square on a skunk), and we passed all three tests. After graduation, the chief called us into his little office and admitted that we had in fact passed in the first course, but he was damned if he would let "five-jump cherries" graduate from his school. Lt. Col. Grange, he said, had agreed with him and thought we'd benefit from an extended Jumpmaster course.

At battalion headquarters, Lt. Col. Grange offered his congratulations. We were now the most experienced parachutist lieutenants in the battalion with more than twenty-five jumps.

Soon after, the battalion had a "Hail and Farewell" gathering where new officers and their ladies were formerly welcomed into the battalion (Hail) and officers leaving the battalion were sent away with appreciation (Farewell). A tradition of the service, it is designed to foster comradery and bonding. It was during this evening that Lt. Col. Grange announced, on formally welcoming me into the battalion, that I was going to be the battalion's reconnaissance platoon leader. That made me something like a scout in the early days of the cavalry, only we would be doing our scouting in the jungles and highlands of Vietnam.

Days later, when the battalion formed up for morning physical training, Grange had me move to the right of the formation and announced we were forming a recon platoon. He asked volunteers for that platoon to move to the right of the formation (where I stood). We had twice as many volunteers as necessary, and it was left to me and my platoon sergeant, Wendell Coursey, to interview the volunteers and make our selections. None of these new troopers had combat experience, so we looked for physical and mental toughness, which we found in abundance. My platoon sergeant and the three NCO (noncommissioned officer) squad leaders we were assigned were all combat veterans from earlier tours in Vietnam.

Lt. Col. Grange convinced the brigade commander, Colonel Larry Mowrey, to send the brigade's reconnaissance platoons to Fort Benning for a one-month mini–Ranger course. I thought to myself, at least this time I'm going back wearing "the tab" and leading troops. Still, it turned out to be almost as hard as the Ranger course itself. It was more than just a four-week tune-up for combat; it was a leadership evaluation as well. After three weeks, our platoon's Ranger department NCO liaison sat me down and explained that the instructors were evaluating the leadership of our platoons. He told me that our platoon was the best and that I was the best of the four platoon leaders (I was one of two who had already earned the Ranger tab). I accepted that compliment for our entire platoon—and that training was a great bonding experience. I remember every soldier of that platoon—most especially those who were later killed in combat—because I selected them to be part of our team.

When we returned to Fort Campbell, we were tremendously confident. A few days before we boarded the C-141 StarLifter to fly to Vietnam, many of the lieutenants had the bright idea to get tattoos. I declined. Grange—who, like me, did not have a tattoo—chuckled at the young lieutenants with their sore and festering arms on the flight over. Tattoos never had any attraction for me. As my platoon sergeant said, noting my lack of one, "Smart move, Lieutenant."

CHAPTER TWO

Vietnam

We flew from Fort Campbell to California's Travis Air Force Base in large USAF C-141 StarLifter aircraft, then to Wake Island for a refuel stop, and finally to Bien Hoa Air Base, just north of Saigon. Never before had most of an army division been moved by air, and it allowed us to arrive in Vietnam in a matter of days, not weeks.

We spent our first night in Vietnam sleeping on the concrete floors of an aircraft hangar, continually awakened by outgoing "friendly" artillery fire. New guys, like me, couldn't yet tell the difference in sound between "outgoing" and "incoming." The veteran sergeants laughed, and said we'd learn soon enough.

Early the next morning, UH-1 Huey helicopters airlifted us to our initial base of operations. It was a base camp near an old French rubber plantation next to the town of Phouc Vinh. South Vietnam's III Corps held this area, which was heavily infested with the enemy. During our stay, we were variously within enemy rocket and mortar fire from War Zone D and the Iron Triangle. We replaced elements of the 1st Infantry Division, the Big Red One, whose division commander, Major General Keith Ware, would be killed months later flying low in his helicopter over the battlefield at Loc Ninh. The division's reputation mirrored that of its commander, a World War II Medal of Honor recipient: fearless.

We lived in large sandbag-fortified tents, sleeping on army cots with mosquito netting hanging over us. The shower water was brackish but wet, and our daily rations included powdered eggs, which I daily declined. We lived as teams, there was no officer housing or NCO housing. I lived with my platoon. The Hilton Hotel it was not.

In early January, we began local tactical operations and by mid-month had full "search and destroy" missions in War Zones C and D. My job, as the battalion's reconnaissance platoon leader, was to find and fix the enemy until larger troop formations could enter the fight.

In mid-January, our battalion was airlifted to Firebase Cahill near War Zone C, a Viet Cong stronghold. The firebase was cut out of the jungle, and its 105mm howitzers, meant to provide fire support, gave us an operational range of about seven miles for our patrols.

The day after we arrived at Cahill, helicopters took us to a small landing zone north of the base, at about the limit of our radio and artillery range. When we went on patrol, I relied heavily on Platoon Sergeant Wendell Coursey, who had been awarded the Silver Star, our nation's third-highest award for valor, for gallantry in action during his previous tour of duty in Vietnam. My point men, Joe Hulse and Kevin Maguire, were the best of the best. Military units are like sports teams; you know when you are good. We were good.

After hitting the landing zone (LZ), we picked up some likely Viet Cong trails, and traveled on a parallel route.

Late into the afternoon, Coursey whispered, "I smell them." Charcoal cooking fires were the giveaway. We were deep in the jungle and forward visibility was limited. We moved slow and cautiously. Suddenly the jungle exploded with Chinese-made Claymore anti-personnel mines. Intense enemy rifle fire cut through the air.

I used the radio to contact the battalion's tactical operations center at the firebase. I yelled to be heard over the gunfire: "Contact! Contact! Contact!" The battalion commander, Lt Col. Grange, was immediately on the radio and I told him we were in a hell of a fight but were holding our own. I told my young radio telephone operator, Dan Close—who by coincidence had gone to high school with my sister in Long Beach, California—to keep the battalion informed, while I led the fight. We were in double-canopy jungle where our gunships and artillery support were next to useless, so I knew we had to fight our way out. By the sheer volume of fire coming at us, I knew the enemy formation was significantly larger than we were. Moving forward, I realized we were on the edge of a line of fortified enemy bunkers. Moving by inches and yards, we fought our way forward. If we got through the first bunker line, we would be inside their perimeter. Outside the bunker line, you just got punished with their interlocking fields of fire. Getting inside would limit their ability to put accurate fire on us. We fought through the first bunker line only to find more bunkers and more interlocking fields of fire. We were in a fight larger than our recon platoon could sustain.

Then Wendell Coursey shouted, "I'm hit!"

"Where?"

"My back!"

I looked—and laughed. An enemy bullet had hit one of his metal canteens, shooting warm water up his back. I told him he was fine, but needed a new canteen.

I knew we had to keep moving, so I yelled, "Stay with me!" as I moved forward with Coursey and my point men, Joe Hulse, Pat Russell, Jimmy Snow, and Dan Close.

By this point, I had already lost two squad leaders (one killed, Staff Sergeant Harold Stanton; and one badly wounded, Staff Sergeant Larry Ferrill, shot in the face and would lose an eye); one point man (Private First Class Kevin Maguire, killed right at the start); and several more troopers (wounded). I radioed Lt. Col. Grange that we were inside the enemy's perimeter, doing well, but in a much bigger fight than anticipated. He said that two rifle companies were heading our way. He told me to break contact and secure a landing zone for their arrival.

We slowly withdrew, not realizing that the enemy was also with-drawing. We moved into a nearby open area, set up a defensive perimeter, and soon had "Hogs," Huey C model helicopter gunships, overhead. Sergeant Pat Russell popped colored smoke to identify the landing zone, and, as expected, enemy gunfire broke out. But it ended as soon as it began, and reinforcements arrived.

Leaping off the lead helicopter was the battalion commander, Lt. Col. Grange. It was the battalion's first fight in Vietnam, and he wanted to be there. Two of the battalion's rifle companies were airlifted in. First to land was Bravo Company, under Captain Freddy Rankin. We had trained a lot with B Company; they were very good and were Lt. Col. Grange's "go to" guys. One of my friends, Joe Hillman, a graduate of North Georgia Military College, was a B Company platoon leader. His platoon was first on the ground. (Months later, Joe was killed leading his platoon in battle. He received a posthumous Silver Star for gallantry in action.)

After the second company was in, Lt. Col. Grange got the leaders together and gave us our instructions. He turned to me and said, "Kel-logg, you guys have done enough and are done for the day." I told him no. We knew where the Viet Cong base camp was and where there was a gap in the bunker line. We also needed to recover the body of Staff Sergeant Harold Stanton, who had been killed in the opening seconds by a Chinese-made Claymore. One-third of my platoon was either killed or wounded, but I knew my men did not want to leave the fight. Their eyes were determined; they wanted to see it through.

By the time we made it to the bunker line, the enemy was gone. They left behind their dead, which was rare; a huge cache of weapons; and food still cooking on the fires. They had left in a hurry.

That night we laagered in the field. Coursey paid me a sergeant's highest compliment: "You did good today, Lieutenant, you did good." His simple words granted me peace of mind that night. I fingered the religious medal attached to my dog tags that I wear to this day: a medal of the Blessed Virgin Mary superimposed on a parachute with the encircling words, "Our Lady Queen of Angels Defend Us in Combat." That day, she had.

Years later, I received an unexpected letter from one of my platoon point men, Pat Russell. Living in Idaho with his wife, he wrote about that day and what it meant to him. I am glad he remembered it. I do too.

We later learned that the enemy we had fought were not mere guerrillas but a veteran Viet Cong main force unit, the thousand-strong Dong Nai Regiment, at a major base camp. They had withdrawn because they were trying to stay concealed from U.S. intelligence. During the Tet Offensive, weeks later, they were one of the main force units attacking the Saigon/Bien Hoa area.

We were sent back to Phouc Vinh to recover and reconstitute the platoon. We had no trouble pulling troopers from the other companies, got back to full strength rapidly, and kept training to stay sharp. Despite local patrolling, the next two weeks were quiet with no enemy contact. This was by the enemy's choice, not ours. Unbeknownst to us, they were preparing for the Tet Offensive, which was to be the turning point of the Vietnam War.

■ ■ ■

For years, the Vietnamese Lunar New Year, Tet, had been observed with an "unofficial" temporary cessation of hostilities. Most South Vietnamese troops went on leave; U.S. forces spent the day grilling hamburgers and hot dogs. In 1968, however, the North Vietnamese and their Viet Cong allies had other plans.

Early on the morning of 30 January 1968, North Vietnamese and Viet Cong troops launched a massive, simultaneous surprise attack on Saigon and more than thirty South Vietnamese provincial capitals. The infamous Tet Offensive had begun. I got an early and unexpected wakeup.

Battalion headquarters was a beehive of activity. Lt. Col. Grange ordered me to lead my platoon to Bien Hoa Air Base, the site of our division headquarters. There was a major firefight near the base. He wanted me to "head to the sound of the guns" and report what was going on. He warned me that we might be on our own for a while.

My platoon saddled up and boarded helicopters. We were inserted where it was assumed the enemy was likeliest to launch their attack on the airfield and division headquarters. We came under enemy fire immediately, with bullets pinging off the Hueys. As we jumped off the helicopters, the rounds were close enough to crack the air, way too close for comfort.

We moved rapidly, passing several dead enemy sappers who had been killed in an earlier failed assault on the airfield. I moved my men into a covered blocking position. We were under constant rifle fire that forced us to crawl the last fifty meters. Facing us was the small village of Dong Lach. The enemy's forces had concentrated there. I radioed Lt. Col. Grange with our position and what I thought was the best path for rifle companies to reinforce us and launch a counterattack. There wasn't much cover available. Captain Freddy Rankin's Bravo Company was again first in. His men moved to link up with the nearby 11th Armored Cavalry (Black Horse) Regiment. Their mission was to assault Dong Lach, reduce the enemy positions, and relieve pressure on the airfield. We had the supporting mission of cutting off any enemy withdrawal from the village.

I radioed for two nearby Cobra gunships to take out a couple of enemy machine gun positions that had us targeted. We popped smoke so the gunships knew where we were, but when the rockets left the gunship tubes, I knew they had targeted us, not the enemy position. I shouted, "Incoming!" and grabbed the radio and dove into a small fold of ground as the rockets exploded around us. I immediately radioed them to cease fire, telling them they had hit us and to clear out; we didn't need any more of their "help." I lost two great young men killed in action due to friendly fire, including Sergeant Phil Germain, the last of my original squad leaders. In thirty days, I had lost them all.

By the end of the day, we had cleared our targets and held the field. Second Lieutenant Sam Galloway from B Company was killed leading his platoon. For his actions, he was awarded the Distinguished Service Cross, our nation's second-highest award for extraordinary heroism. That opening day of the Tet Offensive had been a tough fight. More Distinguished Service Crosses were awarded that day than for any battle in American military history.

Our enemy had been the same Dong Nai Regiment that we had fought earlier—only this time, we eliminated them as a combat force. The fighting we did in Vietnam was at close range, rifle and even pistol range, and I felt no remorse for killing such a brutal enemy. After two days of intense fighting, we were pulled offline and given a rest.

The Tet Offensive proved to be a major battlefield defeat for the enemy. In the following weeks, our troops punished the North Vietnamese regulars and Viet Cong with unremitting attacks as they tried to retreat to their base camps or flee into Cambodia. The Viet Cong were virtually eliminated as a fighting force after Tet, and for the rest of the war North Vietnamese regulars carried the bulk of the fight. We paid a price as well. In the first two weeks of our counteroffensive, one thousand Americans were killed in action and more than six thousand were wounded. Over the course of the next several months, nearly five hundred soldiers would be killed in action each week, and more than 20 percent of the battalion officers I deployed with became casualties, including every other recon platoon leader in the brigade. I was the last recon lieutenant left standing. Our losses were heavy, but the enemy suffered worse, with more than thirty thousand killed or wounded.

Despite the successful results on the ground, what we did not realize at the time was the profound psychological effect the Tet Offensive had on people in the United States, where the media portrayed the enemy offensive as a massive defeat for us and the South Vietnamese. The message was, if we were winning the war, how could this major enemy offensive happen? Were our South Vietnamese allies, caught so apparently unaware, worth the sacrifice of American lives? That message was seemingly affirmed by rising American casualties, terrifying combat footage on American televisions, and the shocking execution of a captured Viet Cong leader by South

Vietnamese national police chief Nguyen Loan. Loan summarily executed the man because he had allegedly led a Viet Cong murder squad and was dressed in civilian clothes rather than in a uniform. But the gruesome visual was captured in a dramatic photo (and video) that stunned the world (and which I never saw until I had returned home from Vietnam).

In Vietnam, occupying terrain or capturing cities and villages did not necessarily equate to "winning," which was why the war was increasingly seen as a war of attrition, where "body counts" of estimated enemy dead became the primary indicator of success. But attrition was a hard way to win, especially when the Communist forces had sanctuaries not only in North Vietnam but also in Cambodia and Laos to which they could retreat, where they could refit, rearm, and then re-enter the fight.

After six months in combat, Lt. Col. Grange called me in. I was now a first lieutenant, and leadership positions in Vietnam rotated every six months. Lt. Col. Grange said it was time to rotate out. Wendell Coursey, my platoon sergeant, had been given a battlefield promotion to second lieutenant and had left the platoon.

Lt. Col. Grange told me I was the brigade's nomination to be the division commander's junior aide. I was not sure what that meant. He said I was going to division headquarters for an interview with the division commander. I packed a bag for an overnight stay, just in case, and flew to division headquarters.

Reporting in to the commanding general's outer office, I sat with several others to be interviewed. There was one nominee from each brigade in the division. When it was my time to be interviewed, I reported in to the division commander, Major General Olinto M. Barsanti. Not large in physical stature but quite large in reputation, Barsanti had been in combat in World War II, Korea, and now Vietnam. No one could question his bravery. He had won the Distinguished Service Cross and had also been awarded five Silver Stars for gallantry in action and six Purple Hearts for wounds received in action. He was a warrior general, and his valorous awards proved it.

His first question was direct: "Why do you want the job?" I told him I didn't. There was a long pause. Then I explained that I had been ordered here by my battalion commander; no one had asked my opinion. There was another long pause—and a long stare—and then a brief discussion about what I had done and where I came from.

As suddenly as the interview had started, it ended. I was told to wait in the outer office until a helicopter could return me to my base camp. Soon the other lieutenants were gone, and I was still waiting. I was surprised when, after a couple of hours, Lt. Col. Grange walked into the office. He said he wanted to talk to me. I said I had told the division commander I didn't want the job. Lt. Col. Grange said Maj. Gen. Barsanti had called him soon after my "interview," and, in a decidedly one-way conversation, proceeded to tell me why I had been nominated. He said I was living on borrowed time, as I should have realized by the fact that I had lost all my original senior NCOs, I was the only original reconnaissance platoon leader in the brigade still alive and not wounded and rotated out, and I had been decorated several times for bravery under fire. The aide position brought recognition and, yes, even honor, to the battalion. He said, "You are a proven fighter and would be associated with a proven fighter in Barsanti and that is what Barsanti wants." He also said, "Barsanti knew he wanted you the moment you said you didn't want the job." Lt. Col. Grange's final comment brought it all home. He said if I came back to the battalion, I would be assigned as the battalion dining facility manager, counting spoons. I got the message. He said, "Go back into Barsanti's office and tell him you would be honored to take the position, if it is still available."

After Lt. Col. Grange left, Maj. Gen. Barsanti called me into his office and asked if I wanted the job. I told him yes and would do the best I could. He laughed and asked about my discussion with Lt. Col. Grange. I told him how much I respected the lieutenant colonel; he was the reason I did not want to leave the battalion. Maj. Gen. Barsanti nodded. "Grange is the best fighting battalion commander in the 101st Airborne Division." He got no disagreement from me—or from the army. Grange retired as a lieutenant general, and the army's best Ranger competition is named after him.

Soon after I took the job with Maj. Gen. Barsanti, we moved our division headquarters to I Corps near the city of Hue. While marines secured the area north of Hue, we performed intensive search-and-destroy missions to the west. We established two large base camps: one to the south and an even larger one to the west, from which we led missions into the twenty-five-mile-long A Shau Valley that bordered Laos, where North Vietnamese forces infiltrated into South Vietnam. In the early days of the war, the army had positioned three Special Forces camps in the valley. But in 1966, the area had become overrun with North Vietnamese regulars, and our small Special Forces units had to withdraw.

The North Vietnamese regulars were much better armed and led than the Viet Cong. They were supported by Soviet-made PT-76 tanks, 85mm Soviet-style field guns, and Chinese-made twin-barreled 23mm anti-aircraft guns, which were very effective against helicopters.

Every day, Maj. Gen. Barsanti, the division command sergeant major George Dunaway (who later became second sergeant major of the army), and I flew over the I Corps tactical zone in Barsanti's UH-1 Huey command aircraft, visiting commanders, overlooking units in action, and inspecting our positions from the South China Sea to the Laotian border. We did not travel with a "chase aircraft," so we had no backup aircraft in the event of an emergency, and part of my job was to keep headquarters aware of our location. We made a large target. No other aircraft in the division had such a giant Screaming Eagle insignia on its nose. And Barsanti liked to fly low, to get a close-up view of the action.

Early in July we flew out to see Lieutenant Colonel "Chargin' Charlie" Beckwith, commanding the second battalion of the 327th Parachute Infantry Regiment. I was shocked when Beckwith looked at me standing next to Barsanti and said, "You look familiar, have we served somewhere together?" I mentioned casually that I had graduated from Ranger school when he commanded the Ranger camp at Eglin in Florida, and let it drop.

As Barsanti and Beckwith were talking, we were suddenly caught in the middle of a firefight. Enemy mortar rounds struck around the perimeter. Barsanti ordered me into the air to locate the enemy. It took us only a few minutes to find the enemy firing positions. They opened up on us with AK-47 rifles and we responded with our M60 machine doorguns. We dispersed them and then called in artillery fire for good measure. The sturdy Huey took a couple of rounds but was fine, and neither I nor any of the crewmen had been hit.

It's not often that a commanding general's aircraft is used as a modified gunship, but that's how Barsanti liked to do things, and it impressed Beckwith. Before Barsanti and I took off again, Beckwith turned to me and said, "Good job, Ranger; I've got a job for you here if you want one." Remembering events in the past, I said nothing. Maj. Gen. Barsanti later awarded me and our four-crew member Huey crew the Air Medal with "V" for valor for our actions that day.

A week later, as we flew low near the A Shau Valley, salvos of enemy rifle fire hit our Huey multiple times, and Maj. Gen. Barsanti was shot through his left calf. When I returned to division headquarters (after getting the general evacuated to the army medical unit at Phu Bai), the division chief of staff, Bill Tallon, asked me what happened. I said, "Sir, don't ask," and he laughed, because he knew exactly what I meant: Maj. Gen. Barsanti was a flying bullet magnet—and he wasn't the only one. A few months later, Major General Keith Ware, the division commander of the 1st Infantry Division, was killed in action when his command-and-control aircraft was shot down. As for Maj. Gen. Barsanti, he was awarded his *seventh* Purple Heart.

Soon after, in a normal rotation of commanders, Barsanti was replaced by Major General Mel Zais, and I was assigned as a Pathfinder platoon leader with the 160th Combat Aviation Group of the 101st Airborne (Air Assault) Division.

The army's first air assault division was the famed 1st Cavalry Division and now the 101st Airborne Division had joined them. Each of the two divisions had an assigned Pathfinder company. The motto of our

Pathfinder company was "First In, Last Out." We led the helicopter assault formations, set up helicopter landing zones for follow-on assault forces, and arranged recovery zones for the extraction of troops.

My first Pathfinder assignment was to lead the way for a massive divisional assault into the A Shau Valley. Two infantry battalions, carried on more than one hundred helicopters, would be our initial lift, with reinforcements to follow. A daylight landing of one hundred helicopters—with gunships and jets in close air support—is hard to miss, but we planned on using multiple landing zones so that we weren't a single target. Nevertheless, every landing came in hot, under enemy fire. As the lifts came in, the enemy fire intensified, and a U.S. Air Force F-4 Phantom providing close air support was shot down by North Vietnamese anti-aircraft fire above the landing zone I was responsible for. As the day wore on, though, the enemy realized that trying to fight it out with us was a losing proposition, and withdrew.

Over the next couple of months, our troops advanced, the enemy retreated, and our assignments involved small unit fighting as a matter of routine.

The "routine" changed when we were charged with making the first night air assault in Vietnam. We had no night vision goggles, no GPS, no advanced avionics, and our target was believed to be a North Vietnamese army stronghold. My Pathfinder team was to set up the landing zone for the initial wave of aircraft.

We used white phosphorous artillery rounds to pinpoint our landing zone and were inserted an hour prior to the assault. We set up lighted "Ts" to indicate touchdown points and then guided the lead assault aircraft in with a shielded, very high-intensity flashlight "light gun" about four feet long. Fortunately, we drew no enemy fire, and the operation proceeded without a hitch. Today, night assaults are routine, but ours was the first, and was done so well that my team was awarded Bronze Star Medals for Meritorious Achievement for a single night mission.

Shortly after that, my tour ended, and I headed stateside. I fully expected, as a regular army officer, that I would be heading back to

Vietnam in a year. So I decided to ask for an assignment on the West Coast, at Fort Lewis, Washington, where I'd be involved in training troops. It was close to home and a nice post. I was ready for a regular bed, regular meals, and a regular existence with no one trying to kill me.

■ ■ ■

I flew home in mid-December 1969 aboard a Pan Am Boeing 707 "Freedom Bird." On lifting off from Tan Son Nhut Air Base in Saigon, the flight was mostly subdued. We refueled once in Japan before landing at Travis Air Force Base in northern California. I spent the evening with relatives in San Francisco and then took a Pacific Southwest Airways flight from San Francisco to Los Angeles/Long Beach and home.

It was a brief visit before I took up my next assignment as a basic training company commander at Fort Lewis, Washington. Training cycles were broken down into physical training, rifle marksmanship, and basic military skills. I sat down with my NCOs and came up with a comprehensive strategy for turning out the best combat-ready soldiers in the brigade. We drilled beyond the normal hours, we were meticulous in teaching the fundamentals of marksmanship, and we were competitive in trying to get better at every aspect of training. We were rewarded with becoming the best training company, not only in the battalion, but in the brigade for eighteen straight months.

I assumed my next rotation would be back to Vietnam, but instead I was sent to Fort Benning and the Infantry Officer Advanced Course. From there I went on to Special Forces training and qualification, which took me to Cambodia, where I was an adviser to the Cambodian army in its fight against Communist forces. As special operations work, it was, technically, covert, and I don't intend to write about it here. Suffice it to say, though, it was among the most interesting and demanding assignments I ever had—at least that I ever had in the jungle.

Much has been written about the lessons of Vietnam, and I am not going to belabor points others have made. I will only say that those of us who stayed in the army after Vietnam had an overriding desire that in all future conflicts we have well-articulated, achievable aims for victory. Limited wars, especially, need well-defined endpoints. In the Vietnam War we were committed to rooting out the Viet Cong, which we achieved, and defending South Vietnam's borders from an aggressive enemy, which meant war without end, until we were withdrawn. By 1973, we had won the war on ground, but the peace agreement relied on our willingness to support South Vietnam and intervene again militarily if the North Vietnamese invaded, as they inevitably did—and we did not respond.

After that I became, of all things, an army recruiter in Phoenix, Arizona.

CHAPTER THREE

A New Army

I immediately liked my new commander, Lieutenant Colonel Charlie Neal, an army aviator. The senior NCO, Master Sergeant Bruce Lavelette, eyed me warily. Lavelette had been an army recruiter for more than fifteen years. This was his area, and it was only because of the army's move to an all-volunteer force that officers were entering these positions, as recruiting had become a high priority. As I discovered when I started meeting my peers, the army wanted some of its best young officers leading the effort; all the recruiting officers I met were combat veterans, highly successful company commanders, and not one of us had wanted to be a recruiter, which is exactly why we were all selected. All of us were given an intensive thirty-day executive sales management course, and while it provided a solid business-like foundation for managing an office, working to meet recruiting goals, and selling what the army had to offer, I still knew next to nothing about the details of recruiting. Master Sergeant Lavelette's experience and guidance proved invaluable.

My recruiting area was the entirety of southern Arizona. Lavelette and I worked hard in this patriotic state, and we soon became the best recruiting area in all of recruiting command, getting big numbers of high-quality recruits.

In early December 1974, Lieutenant Colonel Neal told me I had been selected for early promotion to major and would be sent to the army's Command and General Staff College (CGSC). In those days, early promotions were limited to 2 percent of the force, and selection to CGSC was limited to half of the eligible officer corps; it was a major double coup.

So my next stop was Kansas, where I had a great academic year at the CGSC and continued my studies at the University of Kansas, where I received a master's degree. The army gave me several options for my next assignment, and I chose a position as chief of ground operations at the Support Operations Task Force Europe (SOTFE). Located in Stuttgart, Germany, SOTFE was the Special Operations senior command organization in Europe. These were Cold War days, and the defense of West Germany, and western Europe as a whole, was a major responsibility for the United States Army. We had more than two hundred thousand U.S. Army soldiers stationed in West Germany, and I was somewhat familiar with the country, having been on Special Forces training missions there. Our focus was deterring Soviet aggression, but we had a new challenge as well: terrorism.

In the late 1970s, army Special Forces in Europe consisted of two units: the 1st Battalion, 10th Special Force Group (Airborne) at Bad Tolz near Munich and a very compartmented Special Forces company, the 39th, located in Berlin. In the non-classified world, we just called it "Detachment A, Berlin Brigade." The operators of Detachment A wore no uniforms, followed a "loose dress" policy, and could speak at least one European language fluently. If the Soviets overran Berlin, these highly trained special operators (who looked like civilians) would help lead the resistance.

Berlin was still an occupied city, with Soviet, American, British, and French military zones remaining from World War II. To get to Berlin from western Germany took a minor effort. We had two options: plane or train. Flights had to travel within three narrow flight corridors, each twenty miles wide, and aircraft had to fly at ten thousand feet or lower. The other option was the "duty train" from Frankfurt to Berlin. Run by the U.S. military, it was a good one-time experience...but only one time. The East Germans always ensured there were long travel delays due to "construction" or other events. A normal three-hour rail trip could take up to twelve hours. Time efficient, it was not.

Throughout the U.S. military, Special Forces at the time were regarded as a sideshow. But when Colonel Bill Tyler arrived as our new commander at SOTFE, he brought with him a new attitude about Special Operations. He thought we might have a role to play in preventing terrorism from the Red Army Faction in Germany, the Red Brigades in Italy, and other violent Marxist or pro-Palestinian terrorist groups that were active in Europe. Col. Tyler made me the point man on learning about terrorist threats and working with our allies to see if we could help. The assignment also put me back in contact with Charlie Beckwith, who had just established the 1st Special Forces Operational Detachment Delta, or Delta Force; and we worked together on Special Operations training in Europe.

As it turned out, our major problem was not terrorism in Europe (which the Europeans handled themselves), but turmoil in Iran, where America's ally, Shah Mohammad Reza Pahlavi, had been forced to abdicate. In April 1979, in one of the most consequential developments of our post-Vietnam foreign policy, Iran became an Islamic republic. A former pro-Western bulwark in the region, the Iranian government now turned increasingly hostile to the West. On 4 November 1979, militant Islamist protesters seized the American embassy in Tehran. Sixty-six Americans were taken hostage—and we were facing a crisis.

There was no Central Command at that time, and Iran fell under SOTFE's operational umbrella. If we were called upon to take military action to rescue the hostages, we had an immediate time and distance problem on our hands. I advised Col. Tyler that we needed to work with our friends at Delta Force to come up with some possible plans of action.

Soon joining us in Stuttgart were Jesse Johnson, Delta's deputy commander, and Jerry Boykin, one of Delta's two squadron assault commanders. Meanwhile, the army established a secret task force under Major General Jim Vaught—who had no Special Operations background—to oversee planning for a rescue attempt. Delta Force would take the lead, but SOTFE was involved because assets from Detachment A would be used to infiltrate Iran and act as Delta's advance force. More than a year earlier, Beckwith and I had discussed just this sort of scenario.

The operation became a pickup game with players who had never worked together and now had to perform at the highest level in a complex and dangerous assignment. Planning was fragmented, because of excessive internal secrecy, and flawed because it relied too much on good luck (never a trustworthy planning variable). None of this was compensated for by speed. Months went by and rehearsals were conducted, mostly in the southwest United States. Before the rescue mission was launched, I was rotated to Fort Bragg, and U.S. Marine major Ron Alblowich took my place at SOTFE.

Four months later, in April 1980, Operation Eagle Claw was initiated but then aborted in the Iranian desert, the tragic end coming when one of the mission helicopters collided with another military aircraft. But Eagle Claw's failure set in motion other events that led to the reform of Special Operations.

In December 1980, after a scathing review of Operation Eagle Claw by senior officers (including retired admiral James Holloway, former chief of naval operations), the Joint Special Operations Command (JSOC) was created to bring ground, air, and naval Special Operations assets under one operational command. The creation of JSOC was the pivotal decision in building the U.S. military's Special Operations capabilities—without question, a definite improvement. And in January 1981, the hostages held by the Iranians were released, minutes after the inauguration of President Ronald Reagan. His leadership was a definite improvement too.

■ ■ ■

I was on orders to the army's XVIII Airborne Corps with a follow-on assignment to the legendary 82nd Airborne Division, but on arriving at Fort Bragg I learned that my assignment had been changed. Corps headquarters assigned me to G-3 Operations on the Emergency Deployment Readiness Directorate. The Corps G-3 (operations staff officer) was Colonel Bill Harrison, who would be my direct boss. I was deeply involved in planning training exercises that integrated Rangers, the 82nd Airborne, and Special Operations, and I had a front-row seat for the development of Delta Force. In fact, Beckwith told me, "Go out for Delta selection; you are a good fit."

I asked Col. Harrison about it. He said, "Son, if you do that you will lock yourself in as a special operator and the conventional army track will be behind you. Everybody comes to a fork in their professional career. You just found yours."

Still, I was in great shape and thought I would give it a go, so I applied for the fall selection course and started training for it. But a few months later, Col. Harrison told me there was a new commander of the 1st Brigade of the 82nd Airborne, Colonel Pete Boylan. Knowing that I had arrived at Fort Bragg expecting to join the 82nd, Harrison had arranged an interview for me with the new commander.

Going down to the 1st Brigade headquarters on Ardennes Street, I was confident and prepared. It did not hurt that I was physically hard as a rock from training. Col. Boylan and I hit it off immediately; my thirty-minute interview extended to well over an hour and he offered me the job as his S-3 (the staff officer in charge of training and planning).

I told Col. Boylan I would be honored to be the S-3. The position did not open for a couple of months, so I decided to make the most of the time available to me. I told Col. Boylan that I was slated to go to Delta selection. It was a challenge I didn't want to pass up. But if I passed the course, I would defer an assignment with Delta to be his S-3. He said that was fine and we shook hands on it.

A few weeks later I was heading up to Camp Dawson, West Virginia, for Delta selection. The course puts a premium on mental and physical endurance and the ability to operate alone in a stressful environment. It is tailored after the British SAS course, but I believe is even tougher. Day one included a mountainous twenty-mile night road march with an exceptionally heavy rucksack. It was something of a race, and I came in second. I noticed the instructors weighed and inspected our rucksacks when we got back to camp; anyone missing any items or missing carried weight was dropped from the course.

Each day in the weeks leading up to the final stress week we ran-walked the equivalent of a marathon in the West Virginia mountains and woods: twenty-six miles a day carrying a fifty-pound rucksack, stopping at occasional rendezvous points for the rucksack to be weighed. To me, it was an athletic challenge. One thing I learned later is that any candidate who was a "Victor Whiskey," a voluntary withdrawal, would never be invited back. Going into the final stress week, where we would operate solo in the field, I was in good shape. That week, anyone not reaching various checkpoints by a time clock unknown to us was pulled off the course.

The first day it rained; the second day it rained harder. My feet were badly blistered, and I had the nagging fear that my times were off. At the end of day six, arriving at the last rendezvous point, I was pulled off the course. The next day was the final fifty-mile march, but I would miss it; only two would do it. I was interviewed by the operations team and invited to try again in six months; I was told that those who came back for a second or third try were much more likely to be successful. I told them I didn't have that luxury. I'd made a promise to serve as Col. Boylan's S-3, and I intended to keep it.

The next morning, I flew to Fayetteville, North Carolina. I was barely able to walk off the plane to meet my fiancée, Paige, but I had the satisfaction of knowing that I had given the Delta selection course everything I had. When I got home, I saw that my white socks were stuck to my feet with dried blood from burst blisters. I had to soak my feet in a bathtub before I could peel my socks off. Early the next morning I went to Fort Bragg to see the medics. The overseeing doctor asked me how I'd torn up my feet. "A training event," I said. The doctor was furious and said he needed to report this horrible case of soldier abuse. I told him to relax, it was self inflicted, and made my way out of the medical clinic.

My feet were badly swollen, and I knew I needed to take some leave. (It would be a week before I could put my dress shoes on.) I called my office to make a time-off request. I was told to call the G-1 (personnel officer) of the 82nd Airborne Division. The G-1 was an old Special Forces officer, Jim Guest.

"So, I understand you are not coming to the division," he said.

"What? Where did you hear that?"

"We had a call from DASR in Washington. You're being pulled for a special assignment."

DASR stands for Department of the Army Special Roster and includes all army personnel assigned to special and classified units, including Delta Force. I told him I had no idea what he was talking about. Guest was a well-respected and highly decorated Special Forces officer, who would retire as a two-star general and who knew the community. He said I had better call Charlie Beckwith, who had directed it.

Beckwith was setting up what soon became the Joint Special Operations Command (JSOC), and he wanted me to be one of the original members of the organization. But he had another reason to see me. He had heard what had happened in the Delta selection course and he wanted to give me another shot at it. So here it was again: I had to make a choice between Special Operations and the regular army. Beckwith's offer was tempting, but the next day, I called Col. Boylan, explained my situation, and said my heart was with the 82nd and I wanted to stick with him.

Over the next two years I became the brigade's executive officer, serving under three different brigade commanders. I was selected for early promotion to lieutenant colonel and to the battalion command list. I had gotten to know Jim Lindsay, the division commander, well over the last two years. Known as the "Godfather of the Airborne," he would eventually retire as a four-star general and first commander of the U.S. Special Operations Command. He was a highly visible commander to his men. Every morning, he joined them in their runs down Ardennes Street. Seeing me running with the 1st Brigade staff, he sprinted over next to me and started talking about future assignments. The command slate was getting ready to be published and he said he had a decision to make: who would take command of the 1st Battalion of the 504th Parachute Infantry in the 82nd Airborne, and who would command the Parachute Battalion in Vincenza, Italy? He wanted to know my preference. Both were incredible opportunities and plum assignments.

I told him I would rather stay at Fort Bragg, which pleased him, and he ensured I would command a battalion within our brigade, the "Devils" of the 1st Battalion, 504th Parachute Infantry. The battalion had earned its nickname at Anzio in World War II, where a German officer called its troops "black-hearted devils in baggy pants," and the "Devil" moniker stuck.

■ ■ ■

Over the next two years we gained the reputation as one of the two best infantry battalions in the 82nd. We made a name for ourselves by always training close to the margin: live-fire training, night operations, and being the best shooting battalion not only in the division but in the entire army, winning the All-Army Marksmanship Competition at Fort Benning, Georgia, in rifle, pistol, and machine gun categories two years in a row. Our marksmanship was so good that my master trainer, Randy Rhynes, got assigned to Delta Force. For two years in a row, we won every major competition in the 1st Brigade: best rifle company, best scouts, best anti-armor, best mortars, even best dining facility. Our closest competitor, the 1st Battalion, 505th Parachute Infantry, was commanded by my good friend George Crocker.

The command tour was not without its challenges. In late October, Colonel Hugh Shelton became our new brigade commander (he later became a four-star general and chairman of the Joint Chiefs of Staff). On Monday night, 24 October 1983, my phone rang. I was told to report to my headquarters immediately. There were military police at every major corner and everyone was on the move. I met with Col. Shelton at headquarters, and he told me we would be part of an invasion force against the island of Grenada. Grenada had a Marxist government backed by Cuban Communists and was on the verge of anarchy. While there were greater strategic issues involved, the immediate danger was that American medical students on the island might be at risk.

We were the fifth battalion in the deployment flow. In the morning, we were sitting at the airfield ramp when Col. Shelton drove up, pulled me aside, and said, "The fight in Grenada is almost over. We need to be able to talk and chew bubblegum at the same time."

I knew exactly what he meant. Before this emergency, our battalion had been chosen to represent the 82nd Airborne at a major military exercise, CRISEX, in Spain. We had trained for it and airplanes were coming in the next day. Our place in the Grenada deployment would be taken by another battalion. So we didn't get to fight in Grenada, but we did earn the Spanish parachutist badge.

The flight home was uneventful until we arrived at Pope Air Force Base, where the division commander, General Edward Trobaugh, made a surprise visit to welcome us home. He told me he had just returned from Grenada and said I hadn't missed much. But his kicker comment was, "Paige is doing a great job in Grenada." When I had left for Spain two weeks earlier, my wife, Captain Paige Kellogg, had been at home in Fayetteville. It turned out that the day after I left for Spain she volunteered to go to Grenada as part of the XVIII Corps headquarters. Weeks later, she came home sporting a XVIII Airborne Corps combat patch on her right shoulder. She brought me a Cuban military helmet and a bottle of Cuban rum as souvenirs. I still have the helmet; we drank the rum.

■ ■ ■

Near the end of my command tour of almost three years, Col. Shelton called me into his office and said he had an interesting proposal. A rotation training spot for a battalion had opened at the National Training Center (NTC) at Fort Irwin, California. NTC is a "force on force" training event and is challenging for the very best of units. It is where battalion task forces fight two weeks of war games in the desert against a tremendously talented live opposing force, the 11th Cavalry, known simply in the army as the OPFOR. The OPFOR would use Russian-style tactics and modified tanks and fighting vehicles (to make them look Russian) to bludgeon U.S. units. The success rate in winning against the OPFOR was under 10 percent. You played on their home field and all they did was train for units like yours. The exercise was conducted with observer controllers who evaluated everything a unit did; their after-action reviews bordered on the brutal. Volunteers for this training event were hard to come by because the reputations of units and their commanders were on the line.

The course was designed for tank and mechanized infantry, and no light infantry had ever gone through it. Col. Shelton was blunt. "The stakes for a battalion are high. You will be under intense evaluation. Reports on the outcome will go all the way to the chief of staff."

I said I wanted to do it.

Col. Shelton smiled, picked up his deskside phone, and told Gen. Trobaugh, "NTC rotation: Kellogg wants it." I could tell by the look on the colonel's face that Gen. Trobaugh was thrilled. Whatever training support we needed we'd get. Most units prepare for more than half a year; we had sixty days.

A week later I took the battalion's officers out to the NTC for a ground reconnaissance and to watch a couple of ground battles. It was sobering, especially the regimental attack that overwhelmed the "blue force" unit. The regimental attack is the culminating fight, the Super Bowl of battles at NTC. The OPFOR throws three of their mounted battalions against a single U.S. battalion that is already worn out from almost two weeks of simulated warfare. The attack has simulated artillery, real air support, real CS riot control gas–simulating nerve agents, and a lot of armored vehicles, moving fast. This would be the most challenging training experience we would ever face. My B Company commander, Jim Nordahl, said, "You always talk about high risk; I think we just found higher risk." We trained hard in the subsequent weeks. We studied the OPFOR's strategy and tactics. We pored over after-action reviews. The more I read, the more confident I got. There were flaws, I thought, in the way the OPFOR fought, relying as they did on overwhelming, pounding force—and hubris. The OPFOR was not going to be afraid of a dismounted battalion of infantry; we would take advantage of their overconfidence.

We arrived at Fort Irwin two weeks early to get used to the desert environment and complete our training. I met with one of the senior observer controllers, Lieutenant Colonel P.T. Graney, an experienced armor officer. I liked him. He was no-nonsense and would call it as he saw it. The senior tactical officer, the chief of the operations group (COG), was Brigadier General Wes Clark, a future four-star general and Democratic candidate for president.

We would have one fewer mission than the heavy forces did because of "time-distance" considerations: we walked; they rode. The first two missions involved fixing an enemy force so that a supporting brigade could maneuver and securing a series of mountain passes through which our heavy formations could move. Both times we succeeded in the first part of the mission using night attacks. But as light infantry we could push only so far beyond the passes before the OPFOR could counterattack with overwhelming force. Both missions were "draws" because of our (simulated) losses, but we all became increasingly confident that we could operate successfully in a desert environment. The major fight awaited us.

This was as close to real combat as you could get, and we had proved that the OPFOR was not invincible; we could beat them, at least in a limited area where they couldn't use their massive advantage in mobility and firepower.

Our final mission was to defeat the OPFOR regimental attack. Brig. Gen. Clark was blunt. He gave us no chance of winning. "If the 82nd wins this fight," he said, "it will snow in the desert."

But I believed that, put in the right terrain, we could handle and defeat the OPFOR. We got the right terrain. Our mission was to defend two gaps in the rolling hills of Irwin to prevent the OPFOR from breaking through and attacking the friendly forces to our rear. My assistant division commander, Brigadier General Cal Waller, and my brigade commander, Hugh Shelton, were there to observe as well as the new commanding general of the army's Training and Doctrine Command, four-star general Bill Richardson.

I had my engineer captain build massive anti-tank obstacles with iron tetrahedrons. We dug ditches to slow OPFOR's tanks and carefully positioned our anti-tank weapons to hit their advancing armor from the rear from reverse slope concealed positions.

As dark turned into dawn, we could hear them approaching, hundreds of vehicles. We braced for the "chemical attack," which forced us to fight in protective gear. Our protective masks muffled our voices. We could handle that. What I really wanted was to use the fog of war to muffle the enemy's vision. I wanted to deceive them into believing they had found a weak spot. So, hitting them with artillery, I called for a massive use of green smoke.

In every rotation I'd read about, the OPFOR used green smoke to signify a breach in the opponent's defense. I wanted the OPFOR to mass their forces against that spot. It would allow us to concentrate our fire on them.

The OPFOR commander took the bait, committing his entire force to exploit what he thought was a breach in our defenses; instead, he was funneling his troops into our obstacle-laden kill zone. After two hours the fight was over. Vehicle kills were identified with large flashing lights, and the valley floor looked like a massive Christmas tree. The defeat of the OPFOR regimental attack was complete. And as darkness overtook that late October night, snow fell on the desert.

■ ■ ■

I spent six years at Fort Bragg, and after a brief stint at the Pentagon reporting directly to the army chief of staff on classified programs involving Delta Force and the CIA, and some in-depth study of Afghanistan, I was off to the Army War College.

CHAPTER FOUR

Into Action: Panama and Kuwait

The Army War College was a great break after the Pentagon. Its location in Carlisle, Pennsylvania, was idyllic. The course was designed to give us plenty of free time so we could pursue our own interests. We had classwork Monday through Friday and one twenty-page paper to write. There were a lot of seminars, and we had the opportunity to read more deeply into the profession of arms.

Coming out of Carlisle I knew I wanted to be the G-3 operations officer of an army division. Incredibly, I had a shot at three different army divisions, as the commanders of each had asked for me by name: the 10th Mountain Division at Fort Drum, New York; the 25th Infantry Division in Hawaii; and the 7th Infantry Division (Light) at Fort Ord, California. Even General Lindsay, now XVIII Airborne Corps commander, asked me to come back and be his chief of operations under the Corps G-3. As my wife, Paige said, "We have options." All were good.

I opted for the 7th Infantry Division (Light). It brought me close to home in California and it was a "new" division with a different operational fighting concept.

The army chief of staff, John Wickham, believed the army was too "heavy," depending disproportionally on armor and mechanized units. Wickham believed the army needed lighter formations that could deploy rapidly. Early in his tenure as chief of staff he directed the army to study the concept of a lighter force. The study showed a gap in army capabilities at the lower end of the conflict spectrum. He directed the army to fix it, and the 7th Infantry Division (Light) was born.

Manning the new division with the right people, officers interested in maneuver warfare, was critical. Many officers had been trained to think about pitting massive firepower against the Soviets in Europe. The belief was: if you can fight in Europe, you can fight anywhere. But Wickham knew that Europe was only one theater out of many, with specific strategic and tactical challenges. The 7th Infantry Division (Light) was stocked with Ranger-qualified officers and NCOs, our training was focused on lower-intensity conflicts such as were then happening in Latin America, and our training area was the more than 160,000 acres of Fort Hunter Liggett in Monterey County. After about a year, I was given command of the division's 3rd Infantry Brigade. It also looked like we might be going into action.

In October 1989, Panama's corrupt dictator, Manuel Noriega, survived a coup attempt, and in its wake some worried that he might grow more aggressive and threaten the Panama Canal and the U.S.-occupied Canal Zone. President George H.W. Bush had made it clear that we would maintain stability in the area. As part of that effort, the 7th Infantry Division (Light) would station one of our battalions and a brigade headquarters at Fort Sherman on the Atlantic side of the canal. My brigade's six-month rotation into the Canal Zone would begin in late October.

The tension in Panama was palpable. A week after our arrival, General Max Thurman became the commander of U.S. Southern Command in Panama. I told my operations officer, Major Greg Gardner, "We will be in a fight in less than two months."

Gen. Thurman, a former 82nd Airborne Division artillery commander, visited us the day after he took command. Accompanied by his exceptionally talented chief of operations, Brigadier General Bill Hartzog, he gathered my small command group into a conference room and said, "Be ready." Walking out, Hartzog grabbed my arm and said, "Be REALLY ready." I got the message. The fight was just around the corner.

Gen. Thurman was a no-nonsense commander who had taken over from General Fred Weyand. He represented our new aggressive approach to Noriega. Gen. Weyand had been cautious, to the point of continually apologizing for the Noriega regime. Just a week earlier he had told me, in his conference room in Panama City, that Noriega could not be defeated; his grip on the country was too great. Gen. Thurman better reflected my own thinking on Panama—if Noriega threatened our interests, he would meet his match.

Gen. Thurman asked me to design and conduct training exercises that would demonstrate our right to defend the Canal Zone as covered under the Panama Canal Treaty. I added another wrinkle: we would use the exercises as ground reconnaissance missions against potential targets. As German field marshal Erwin Rommel said, "Time spent in reconnaissance is seldom wasted."

On 15 December 1989, Noriega announced that Panama was in "a state of war with the United States." He said our military exercises amounted to "constant psychological and military harassment" and were "insulting" Panamanian "sovereignty and territorial integrity." Some blew this off as mere rhetoric, but a day later, Noriega made his fatal mistake.

On 16 December, Marine first lieutenant Robert Paz and two military buddies were heading to a restaurant for dinner. They made several wrong turns and ended up at a checkpoint manned by Panama Defense Forces and militia. The Panamanian guards harassed them, and the driver, a fellow Marine officer, thought they might be in a trap. He tried to gun the car to safety, and the Panamanian forces opened fire, wounding the driver and killing Lieutenant Paz. A U.S. Navy officer and his wife, stopped at the same checkpoint, were witnesses. They were arrested by the Panamanians. The officer was badly beaten. His wife was threatened with rape.

When informed of this, President Bush had had enough. The fight was on; Noriega just didn't know it yet.

My secure telephone rang. It was Brig. Gen. Hartzog.

He said, "Are you guys ready?"

"Yes...for what?"

"H-Hour 0100/20 December."

The invasion of Panama was based on a sophisticated plan involving an 82nd Airborne brigade, the entire 75th Ranger Regiment, Delta Force, Navy Seal Team Six, and other units hitting more than two dozen targets simultaneously, at night. My brigade, Task Force Atlantic, had nine targets and thousands of Americans to protect. Gen. Thurman told me in our final briefing, "Kellogg, you lose one American and you have failed."

Inevitably, "friction" enters the best-laid plans, and last-minute changes meant that, among other complications, the 82nd Airborne would arrive late (because of weather) and I would have only half my expected strength available for one of my assignments, which was freeing the political prisoners at Renacer Prison. Briefing him on my assault plans, I told Lieutenant General Carl Stiner, XVIII Airborne commander and the operational commander of the invasion, that every single unit of mine was committed. I had no reserve to try to stabilize a bad situation or exploit a success. Lt. Gen. Stiner said, "I know, Keith. You will be on your own."

There's an old adage that no battle plan survives first contact. We were about to prove it again, in spades, but that's what happens when you try to take down an entire country in one night. In their book *Operation Just Cause: The Storming of Panama*, Thomas Donnelly, Margaret Roth, and Caleb Baker note, "Nowhere in Panama were U.S. forces as fragmented at H-Hour as in Kellogg's area of operations. His Task Force Atlantic waged assaults over an area of 1,800 square kilometers, including five PDF [Panama Defense Forces] installations and the Madden Dam, a strategically vital target." Fragmented we might have been, but I intended to bring some cohesion by being in the field with my men, moving from target to target.

Lifting off from Fort Sherman at midnight in our command-and-control helicopter, we linked up with the small air column flying down the canal towards Renacer Prison. Our night vision goggles combined with navigation lights on the canal made it look like a bright super-highway. We had planned on the prison's lights illuminating the landing site for our helicopters, but when our Cobra gunships engaged the guard towers, they also managed to shoot up the generator, and everything went dark. To their credit, the helicopter pilots pushed through. We achieved total surprise, our assault force was on the ground, and in minutes we had control of the prison.

By early morning, we had hit each of our targets—and done so successfully. We "owned" our part of the canal; had cordoned off its major city, Colon; and Seal Team Six was on the hunt for Noriega. I was preparing for the day's operations when Division Commander General Carmen Cavezza called. "Keith, your father died earlier tonight." A sledgehammer into the chest. I was stunned. He said, "I am ordering you home. There is a flight in the morning, and I want you on it." I went back to my room and just looked at the wall. I finished the planning for the assault into Colon, and the next day led our troops as we cleared Colon of enemy forces and successfully took down all our assigned targets.

We had done our job. I had lost one soldier killed in action and seventeen wounded. It was an incredible success. Meticulous planning and violent execution of our plans made the difference. But I had to face one very mad division commander, because I had disregarded his order and missed my flight.

At Fort Sherman, I saw the commanding general's helicopter and Gen. Cavezza standing near it. He said, "You know, I should relieve you for violating a direct order. I told you to fly back to the States." I told him I had now accomplished every mission I and my task force had been given; I couldn't have left before then.

Apparently, he wasn't that mad. Not long after, he sat on the promotion board that recommended me for promotion to brigadier general and relayed my new assignment as chief of staff to the 82nd Airborne Division at Fort Bragg.

■ ■ ■

Shortly before my departure to Fort Bragg, Iraq invaded and occupied Kuwait and threatened Saudi Arabia. Iraq had the world's fourth-largest army, and if it seized the major Saudi Arabian oil fields, it would directly control 20 percent of the world's oil supply and dominate the Persian Gulf.

President George H.W. Bush had just announced, "At my direction, elements of the 82nd Airborne are arriving today to take up defensive positions in Saudi Arabia." The entire 82nd Airborne Division was getting ready to deploy—and I was still in California. We had two cars, two kids, and two dogs. And one of the kids had chicken pox. Oh, and my wife was expecting as well. But she knew what I had to do and encouraged me to do it.

I hopped a flight from Travis Air Force Base to Fort Bragg. Arriving at headquarters, I met with Major General Jim Johnson. I'd known him for years. He was a tall, fit, fighting soldier who ran six miles every day. He told me I hadn't missed anything; no one had yet deployed.

"But sir," I said, "the president was on television. He said we were there already."

Maj. Gen. Johnson said, "A little disinformation doesn't hurt."

In truth, the first parts of the division would head out the next day. Maj. Gen. Johnson told me I would not be deploying until my family was safely settled at Fort Bragg. In the meantime, there was plenty to do. The military was chartering passenger aircraft to move troops and using military aircraft to move equipment.

We pushed as hard as we could on the deployment sequence. Every day mattered and getting some level of troop strength on the ground in

Saudi Arabia was critical. Nearby Pope Air Force Base had civilian and military aircraft landing and departing hourly.

Twenty-four hours after my wife, Paige, arrived with our son, Bryan, and daughter, Meaghan, I was off. I told them I would be back in sixty days. Turned out I was optimistic. It was more like 220 days.

Landing in Dhahran, Saudi Arabia, in August is like being in an oven turned up high. Average temperatures were well over one hundred degrees and air conditioning was a rare commodity. We established our division headquarters, Champion Main, just north of Dhahran in a new but unoccupied Saudi Air Defense base. Our headquarters was crammed, we worked around the clock, and we slept in our offices.

The 82nd Airborne straddled the one major north-south road from Kuwait. The terrain was flat, and we had no withdrawal plan. Our role was to delay any enemy advance as long as possible.

Reinforcements were on the way, including the 101st Airborne Division. We also had excellent intelligence and exceptional satellite imagery of the Iraqi forces—armored and mechanized divisions among them—pointed against us. The Iraqis had a tremendous numerical advantage, but they didn't use it, worried perhaps that their armor would be countered by our air power but also with the knowledge that the 82nd would fight and fight hard. And while they waited, the odds shifted in our favor. When the 1st Cavalry Division began off-loading M1A1 tanks, the best in the world, I knew we had passed our most dangerous phase. The Iraqis would not attack, but nor would they withdraw; in the meantime, President Bush was putting together an impressive international coalition to repel the Iraqi invasion of Kuwait. By December 1990, we had six heavy divisions on the ground, counting a British armored division. We also had, separately, two U.S. marine divisions and one French division. To use a popular phrase, we were loaded for bear. This was not a defensive build-up. It was an offensive force to drive the Iraqis out of Kuwait.

The United Nations Security Council authorized the use of "all necessary means" against Iraqi forces if they did not withdraw from

Kuwait by 15 January 1991. As preparation, we began moving into our assault locations in early January. But just before that I was blessed with the news that my son Tyler was born. In our planning, some of our casualty projections were very high, and we assumed the Iraqis might use chemical weapons, as they had against Iran in the Iran-Iraq War of 1980 to 1988.

Before the ground campaign, the Iraqi Army was subjected to six weeks of U.S. Air Force pounding. On 24 February, we crossed the border into Iraq. We achieved near-total surprise; the enemy hadn't realized that our lines extended so far west.

Four days after we crossed into Iraq, the war was over. General Colin Powell, chairman of the Joint Chiefs, had said in an earlier press conference, "Our strategy to go after this army is very, very simple. First, we're going to cut it off, and then we're going to kill it." That was exactly what we did, defeating the world's fourth-largest army in four days.

After the Vietnam War, many of us involved in the nation's military affairs wanted to ensure that in any future use of military force, if we were committed to fight, we would fight to win. And that is precisely what we did in Panama and the Arabian desert. President George H.W. Bush, though granted only one term as commander in chief, proved in this regard to be a worthy successor to President Ronald Reagan.

In a little over a year, I had been in two fights on two different continents: one a low-intensity conflict in Panama where our light, deployable forces were the key element, and one in the Middle East where our heavy armored forces with massive air support carried the day. In both cases, we had achieved total victory. Those of us who had stayed in the army after Vietnam had made it better. We were determined to recreate a proud, dominant, winning military—and we had been vindicated.

CHAPTER FIVE

Generalship in Peace and War

A fter Operation Desert Storm, I returned to Fort Bragg for about a year, before I was given yet another significant assignment: commanding general of Special Operations, Europe (SOCEUR). SOCEUR was the Cadillac of Special Operations Command. I had Army Green Berets, Navy SEALs, and U.S. Air Force MC-130 Combat Talons and HH-53 Pave Low helicopters all under my operational control.

With the collapse of the Soviet Union, my command responsibilities and our training areas extended to Eastern Europe and Africa. Our rapid deployment capabilities meant we were the first call when the U.S. commander in Europe needed something done. In late October 1992, for instance, I was told, "I need you to pull the ambassador and his staff out of Tajikistan." Ambassador Stanley Escudero and his staff were stuck in the middle of a civil war.

I alerted a small Special Forces team and we loaded onto a U.S. Air Force C-141 and headed east. We made our plans in-flight to the point of receiving airspace permission minutes before crossing over into the airspace of different countries. When we reached the airfield in Tajikistan's capital, Dushanbe, we could hear explosions in the distance. Linking up with Russian forces on the airfield, I used very broken college Russian, and the Russian commander used very broken English, to get us to the ambassador's location. We found Ambassador Escudero and his staff waiting for us at the main airport terminal, loaded them up, and prepared to take off for Ramstein, Germany. Right before we left, a staff officer from the State Department said, "Sir, we are allowed to take the people but not their pets." I told him what he could do with the regulations and that we were taking "people, poodles, and parakeets." I'd let customs figure it out later—and it all turned out fine.

Our next big call was to help out the United Nations Protection Force (UNPROFOR), which had its hands full with the civil war in Bosnia.

U.S. aircraft were not allowed in Bosnian airspace, so we flew into Sarajevo on a Russian Ilyushin II-76 with UN insignia and a Russian crew. After flying on Russian aircraft with Russian crews (who on our return journey transported damaged vehicles that were leaking fuel—and smoked cigarettes around them) I will never, ever, bad-mouth a U.S. Air Force plane or crew. French paratroopers met us at Sarajevo's battle-scarred airport and loaded us into armored vehicles. The headquarters of the United Nations commander, French general Philippe Morillon, was a few miles away. Travelling down the highway, I kept hearing "pings." The French paratrooper who was driving told me not to worry: "They are just playing around, shooting at us." The circular blue United Nations logo on the side of the vehicle made a perfect, tempting target; the vehicle's armor, however, also offered near-perfect protection.

My assignment here was to assess the situation and figure out how we might be able to help. Sitting at a formal dinner that night with Gen. Morillon's team, our discussions were interspersed with the background noise of mortar fire. Gen. Morillon explained that he was cut off in Sarajevo. He had no forward liaison teams and not even a satellite communications link to his headquarters in Paris. I was shocked. The next day we were taken around the city. It was sobering. The city's 1984

Olympic stadium and the surrounding area was a giant cemetery. The Bosnian Serb artillery on the surrounding hills had made the city of Sarajevo a killing ground. I gathered what intelligence I could and assumed that though the United States wanted Europe to handle this problem I knew we would soon be involved.

That proved to be the case two years later, in 1995, after Bosnian Serbs massacred eight thousand Bosnian Muslim men and boys. Nearby Dutch forces did not intervene. Within months, a NATO peacekeeping force, with U.S. troops, entered Bosnia. My command, with robust support from U.S. Special Operations Command, provided significant special operations and search-and-rescue support from a deployed forward operational base at Brindisi, Italy.

My last big event at SOCEUR was in late July 1994, when we deployed Special Operations forces to keep the airport of Rwanda's capital city, Kigali, open during the Rwandan Civil War, so we could deliver relief supplies.

After my European stint, I returned stateside to Fort Monroe, Virginia, and the army's Training and Doctrine Command, where I was reunited with General Bill Hartzog, my old battle buddy from Panama. Gen. Hartzog wanted me to lead the effort to "digitize the army." Calling it Force XXI, we applied Information Age technology to improve our operational fighting force.

I noticed during this period that Gen. Hartzog was always reading science fiction novels. I finally asked him why, and he said, "Futures: a lot of what you read in science fiction later becomes reality." He was right—and some of those novels have ended up on the army's required reading list. Robert Heinlein's 1959 novel *Starship Troopers* is a good example. In that book you'll read about infrared technology, night vision goggles, and satellite communications long before we had them.

Force XXI worked and senior officers noticed. It propelled me to my next assignment, one very few are privileged to get.

■ ■ ■

After I was promoted to two-star general, I was given the opportunity of a lifetime: command of the 82nd Airborne Division at Fort Bragg. I loved every minute of it. I joined the troopers in jumping out of airplanes. I joined them in their morning runs on Ardennes Street and in tough field training. And with the leaders I had, the division could have run on autopilot, but we worked hard to keep it ready to deploy and fight if needed. My only regret was that I didn't get to fight with the division. But I knew when I left that they were more than ready if called upon.

My next stop was the Pentagon. I served as the assistant operations officer for the army. As one of the "Three Wise Men" of the army—the other two being the army's budget officer and the programmer of the army—we had to have detailed knowledge on every program in the army, as we were the last stop for recommending technology and programs to senior leadership. Having oversight of billion-dollar programs—dozens of them—was mind-numbing and tedious. By the end of each week, I didn't feel "wise," I felt wasted. Some people like this sort of work; I'm not one of them.

One night, sitting at home in my quarters at Fort Myer, Virginia, we heard a knock on the door. In walked the chairman of the Joint Chiefs, Hugh Shelton, who lived just a block away. A chairman of the Joint Chiefs doesn't just drop in on you; something was up. When he said, "Sit down," I thought, "So this is how you get fired; I guess my unhappiness in crunching budget numbers has shown through." Instead, he said, "I have a proposition for you. I want you to become the Joint Staff J-6"— that is, the director for Command, Control, and Communications for the Joint Chiefs of Staff, to give the job its official title. I would report directly to him. It was an honor—but an infantryman as a senior communications guy? Well, I can't say it made sense to me at the time, but who was I to say no?

Getting promoted to three-star general and moving to the Joint Staff had me feeling like a second lieutenant again. I had a ton to learn. But my crash course was soon interrupted by another crash, a deadly one that changed everything.

■ ■ ■

I woke up early on 11 September 2001 for my morning run. I had a speech to give later that day to the Armed Forces Communications and Electronics Association at Fort Monmouth, New Jersey, and wanted to get my run in early so I could push some paperwork before my departure. My flight from the Pentagon helicopter pad was set for eleven o'clock. The morning was bright. A good day for flying, I thought.

A little before nine, my executive officer, Tracy "Moose" Amos, came into my office, turned on the television, and said, "Sir, you have to see this." A commercial airliner had crashed into the World Trade Center's north tower. As we watched the replay, it was beyond our comprehension. How, on such a clear day, could that happen? Minutes later, the south tower exploded in fire as well. I initially thought a circling helicopter had crashed into it and then I saw that replay. A second large aircraft came into the picture. Watching it hit the south tower, I knew this had been no accident.

I immediately moved to the National Military Command Center (NMCC) directly across from my office. The NMCC is the military's global command center, with information feeds from everywhere in the world and from places and agencies you might otherwise only read about in novels. Marine lieutenant general Greg Newbold as the Joint Staff J-3 operations officer was responsible for NMCC operations; I was responsible for NMCC communications. Our offices were side by side, and we could be in the command center in seconds, but Greg was gone that day, so I took a more aggressive role inside the center. I immediately checked the status of the NMCC watch teams that tracked everything from intelligence to media reports, but my first real intelligence came from my executive officer, who confirmed that "a big airplane" had crashed into the Pentagon. I was joined in NMCC by Vice Admiral Scott Fry, the director of the Joint Staff and senior staff officer in the NMCC. The chairman of the Joint Chiefs, General Hugh Shelton, was halfway across the Atlantic en route to the United Kingdom for a conference, but the vice chairman of the Joint Chiefs, General Dick Myers, soon arrived and became the senior officer in the command center. I briefed him on everything we knew so far, which was not much. Gen. Myers said, "Where's the secretary of defense?" I told him we had no idea. We did know that the Pentagon had been struck on the army staff and navy operations center side, and though we had not felt the impact on our side of the Pentagon, we could already smell smoke from the fires now raging.

A short time later, Secretary of Defense Donald Rumsfeld appeared. He looked a little disheveled, but that was because he had gone immediately to the attack site to help remove casualties. Gen. Myers told him bluntly that we needed him in the NMCC, not as a stretcher bearer. The country was at war, but we didn't know with whom. We had already alerted President George W. Bush. We were also talking directly to Vice President Cheney and Condoleezza Rice, the national security adviser, in the presidential bunker (also known as the Presidential Emergency Operations Center) underground at the White House. General Shelton was rerouting his flight back to Washington, but he was still hours away from arrival.

The chief of naval operations, Admiral Vern Clark, and his vice chief, Admiral William "Fox" Fallon, rushed in and told us that the crashed plane had taken out their naval command center. It was our "holy crap" moment.

We knew another aircraft, United Airlines flight 93, had been hijacked and was heading for Washington, D.C. We still had no idea who had planned and initiated these attacks, but they were clearly coordinated. They had hit the economic center of America in the World Trade Center next to Wall Street. They had hit our nation's military headquarters at the Pentagon. We had to assume the worst. There was at least one hijacked plane heading for Washington—and there could be others. The likely targets had to include the Capitol and the White House.

Rumsfeld was on a speakerphone with Vice President Cheney, who said, "You are weapons free over Washington." The room went dead quiet. Those words meant the military had authority to shoot down anything flying over Washington, D.C., including any commercial airliner. The Federal Aviation Administration had ordered all U.S. airspace closed and all flights grounded. Control of the air now belonged to the Defense Department. We alerted Andrews Air Force Base. Their Air National Guard fighter jets took to the skies, but were not armed. Armed F-16s, however, took off from Langley Air Force Base in southern Virginia and were given the mission of providing a fighter cap over Washington, D.C. That's when we learned that United 93 had crashed in Pennsylvania at 10:04 a.m. It was only later that we learned that Flight 93's heroic passengers had saved the Capitol. Our armed intercept fighters would not have arrived in time.

As all this was going on, the Russians were conducting a significant military exercise involving not only conventional, but also nuclear forces. I recommended to Secretary Rumsfeld that we should get on the hot line and tell the Russians we were raising our Defense Condition, or DEFCON, from "4," which is normal status, to "3," which is increased readiness. Just raising it one level would get everyone's attention. If you go to "2," nuclear weapons are loaded on board the bombers, and at "1" you are either in or nearing military operations. Rumsfeld told his Russian counterpart, Defense Minister Sergei Ivanov, that the United States was under attack. We did not yet know from whom or if this was a precursor to a larger attack or a "decapitation attack" designed to take out U.S. senior leadership. In either case, we were prepared for war.

Everyone was calm. Ivanov had known only what he was picking up on global television feeds, and he appreciated the update. Almost immediately after the call, Russia lowered its military posture and ended their major exercise It was a clear statement: "It wasn't us."

The 11 September 2001 terrorist attacks on the United States claimed the lives of three thousand people; 125 of those were at the Pentagon, including my friend Lieutenant General Tim Maude, the Army's personnel chief and the senior military officer killed that day. In the aftermath, I became the Joint Staff's liaison with FBI headquarters, charged with integrating, coordinating, and streamlining communications among government agencies. I worked with a brilliant, if very eccentric, information technology leader and retired MIT professor at the Cambridge Technology Group in Boston, Professor John Donovan. Our two staffs created a program called the Joint Protection Enterprise Network (JPEN) that would immediately share anti-terrorism and force protection information across all agencies, something we were lacking on 9/11. It took us ninety days to develop and sixty days to make operational at thirty U.S. sites. General Dick Myers later said of JPEN, "This is too good to be true and it works." It was a great example of a successful private-public partnership in time of need, something I would see on a greater scale almost twenty years later.

I remained with the Joint Staff through the beginning of the war in Afghanistan and the Second Gulf War. Stuck in staff work, and without a command assignment awaiting, I decided to move on. I had loved every minute of my military career, but now it was time to do something different. It was time for a second career—one where I could serve my country a new way.

■ ■ ■

I had just settled into a really good civilian executive management position with Oracle Corporation when I got a call, in late September 2003, from General Myers, by then chairman of the Joint Chiefs, and Paul Wolfowitz, the deputy secretary of defense. Gen. Myers said, "Can you come in tomorrow for a discussion on Iraq?" I said sure and met with them in the chairman's office early the next day.

Gen. Myers said, "Would you go to Iraq and be the chief operating officer for the Coalition Provisional Authority?"

The CPA, led by Ambassador Jerry Bremer, was the transitional government of Iraq created in May 2003. Because the CPA was a Defense Department organization, Bremer theoretically reported to the secretary of defense. However, he had the title of U.S. presidential envoy and administrator in Iraq, and he took that to mean that he reported to the president. Rumsfeld, Wolfowitz, and Myers wanted someone to rein Bremer in and keep communications lines open with the Pentagon staff. I would be that someone.

My answer was, "No."

Wolfowitz said something about recalling me to active duty. I told him what he could do with that idea.

That night I told my wife, Paige, about the meeting. She brought me up short. "You personally know every senior military commander on the ground. You can work with them. You can help. You should go."

I conceded that she was right. But I saw the occupation of Iraq for what it was: a mess.

The next morning, I spoke with Myers and Wolfowitz.

"Okay," I said, "I'll do it. But I have two conditions."

The first was that I had to get permission from Oracle's CEO, Larry Ellison. After all, I had just come on board at his company; I had great respect for him and Oracle's president, Safra Catz; and they had entrusted me with work on important homeland security issues. Wolfowitz said he knew Ellison and would make that call.

My other condition was that I take an operations team with me. Neither Wolfowitz nor Myers had an issue with that.

The first calls I made were to a retired army major general, Jim Jackson, who was then working at the research and technology firm Battelle, and Major Bert Ges, then an observer controller at the army's National Training Center and my former aide in the 82nd. In fewer than ten minutes, both were on board.

The third officer I brought on the team was future three-star general Mike Oates, the executive officer to the secretary of the army. I told him I wanted thirty of the best officers in the Pentagon; he found them and we got them.

I knew we had a tough assignment, but it was only once I was in Baghdad, weeks later, that I realized just how tough. On my first day in country, I went to a meeting between Ambassador Bremer and the Iraqi Governing Council. The council consisted of twenty-five Iraqi political and tribal leaders Bremer had appointed to help him govern. If this was the government of Iraq, we were screwed. There was little, if any, consensus, which meant that little, if anything, constructive would get done, at least not quickly. Dissension in Iraq was mirrored at home, where Secretary of Defense Donald Rumsfeld and Secretary of State Colin Powell constantly sniped at each other about Iraq (and everything else). Bremer did his best, but his authority was inadequate. The situation in Iraq, I thought, required a strong man, not a committee led by a diplomat. We should have handled the occupation of postwar Iraq as we handled the occupations of Japan and Germany after World War II. In Japan, General Douglas MacArthur was the supreme commander of all the Allied forces and determined how Japan would be governed. In Germany, General Lucius Clay acted as military governor. Both were brilliant administrators and understood complex organizations.

Bremer had been the ambassador to the Netherlands for three years. That was the depth of his organizational skill and experience. I concluded that no one in senior echelons, from the White House to the Pentagon, had thought about what Iraq would look like after the war. It appeared that everyone thought after the fighting we would just go home. Iraq's new government would be entrusted to talented expatriates schooled in republican government, or to Iraq's own emerging Jeffersonian Democrats—only there weren't any, or certainly not enough to matter. Rumsfeld wanted us out of Iraq as quickly as possible. I could see why. But I am a big believer that if you break something, you are obligated to fix it. And we really broke some stuff. And it wasn't even so much the war that broke things; it was the "peace," where we made things infinitely harder for ourselves.

Bremer arrived in Iraq on 12 May 2003. Within four days he had issued two extremely consequential orders. The first was that all members of the ruling Ba'ath Party be removed from government leadership and management positions. The second order disbanded the Iraqi military and security infrastructure. Welcome, then, to governmental chaos and a ready-made insurgency.

My team focused on revamping the security forces, rebuilding a broken oil industry, and power generation. After several months, I returned home, knowing that we had done all we could do, giving the CPA a strategic plan for moving forward. Wolfowitz wanted me to stay, but I was done. Our troops had done a great job winning the war. But our foreign policy "experts" had failed catastrophically in not having any practical, realistic strategic vision for the aftermath—and we're still paying a price for that. My opposition to the foreign policy mandarins who made such grievous mistakes in Afghanistan and Iraq was one very big reason for the eventual, somewhat unexpected, turn in my career.

PART TWO

A POLITICAL LIFE

CHAPTER SIX

Candidate Trump

I spent the next twelve years in business and had a good run of success. But the time had come for a new challenge. In late October 2015, I had breakfast with General Jack Keane, then a Fox News contributor. The presidential campaign season was getting started, and he asked me if I'd ever thought about advising a political candidate on national security. "If you're interested," he said, "I know some of the candidates, and would be happy to connect you." I told him there was only one candidate who interested me: Donald Trump. He was the only outsider of the bunch. He spoke his mind—and I liked what he said. I agreed whole-heartedly with his America First agenda. Though a brash New Yorker, Trump had the political views of patriotic heartland America: restoring American jobs, ending unnecessary wars, enforcing our immigration laws, and appointing judges who followed the Constitution and didn't legislate from the bench. General Keane didn't know anyone in Trump's orbit, but that conversation got me thinking. I thought Trump had sound instincts and the right ideas, but, as a businessman, he was new to for-eign policy and defense issues. Perhaps I had something to offer him as a national security adviser.

I made cold calls to the campaign, to Rudy Giuliani's office, and to Governor Chris Christie's office. I paid a visit to Jeff Sessions's office and met with Pete Landrum, a reserve Special Forces officer who worked for Sessions and told me he would circulate my name to the campaign. I left a phone message for Sam Clovis, who, I learned, was a leading figure on the campaign. But I didn't seem to be getting anywhere.

Then, one Saturday morning in late December 2015, my phone rang. It was Sam Clovis. Sam is a gregarious guy and a former air force fighter pilot. After sharing a few war stories to break the ice, I told him how hard it was to get in contact with anyone on the campaign, and he just laughed and said, "Well, we are not a traditional campaign." Sam said he had done a background check on me. He thought I'd be a good fit for the campaign and that Trump might like to tap my experience.

That was more flattering than I knew, because the Trump campaign was designed to be small and frugal, not top heavy with advisers, consultants, and pollsters. The campaign was meant to be efficient, agile in responding to the news, and innovative in willing to try new approaches in policy and communications. The few of us who were there at the beginning saw the campaign as a populist crusade—and we were convinced that against all odds we could win. Still, in the early weeks, through the Iowa caucuses and New Hampshire primary, I did little but watch, like everyone else did. It was all about on-the-ground retail politicking, and the candidate had no need to consult me on national security or foreign policy details. It was only when the campaign prepared for the South Carolina primary that Sam called me and asked whether they could publicly release my name as a national security adviser to Trump. I said he absolutely could. This was no small thing, because Trump was facing extraordinary levels of opposition vitriol, and anyone who came out supporting him could expect the same.

The campaign had a spartan headquarters in Trump Tower. Corey Lewandowski, the campaign manager, was focused on accumulating delegates. Senator Jeff Sessions, the senior elected Republican who was a prominent Trump supporter, provided political insight. I talked with them whenever they had a question about national security policy, but my role was very much behind the scenes.

That changed on 21 March 2016 because of a story in the *Washington Post*. In a meeting with the *Post*'s editorial board, Trump had named his campaign's five national security advisers; I was one of them and knew only one of the others, anti-terrorism expert Walid Phares. I had never heard of Carter Page or George Papadopoulos, and though Joe Schmitz had worked at the Pentagon, I was not familiar with him. I later learned that this team, which would be slightly expanded, had been assembled by Sam Clovis. I had to confess that it didn't seem like much of a team. But the immediate issue for me was how I should respond to the press. I called Hope Hicks and told her, "Benjy Sarlin from MSNBC is loading up my voice mail. He wants to talk with me. I need your guidance." Hope said, "It's fine to talk with him; just stay in line with Trump's positions." That was not hard. Candidate Trump and I agreed on every issue.

I talked with Benjy the next morning. It was my first official discussion with a reporter while part of the campaign. Much of that conversation was about what the campaign meant by promoting a policy of America First. I argued that it was not about isolationism or unilateralism. It was simply about making America's national interests the top priority of America's government—putting that ahead of any ideological commitment to global liberalism in terms of trade policies, foreign policies, or any other policies. That struck me as common sense. But, like everything else about the Trump campaign, the idea of America First drew the ire of many prominent people. In fact, I found that my association with Donald Trump was akin to being diagnosed with typhoid fever. I heard that people I was associated with in the business world no longer wanted anything to do with me.

But as Trump became the presumptive nominee, the campaign began acquiring some establishment support, including from veteran political operative Paul Manafort, who volunteered his services to Trump in late March and was named campaign convention manager.

Within weeks, the original campaign manager, Corey Lewandowski, was out of a job. Manafort himself lasted only until the end of the summer, and after his departure, he was not missed. He and seasoned pollster Kellyanne Conway pushed hard for Mike Pence, then governor of Indiana, to be Trump's pick for vice president. That was good advice, and while Manafort knew a lot about politics, it was obvious to me that he was not interested in anything involving "national security," which I assume he considered electorally irrelevant. He also didn't know anything about effective management. He did things the Washington way, running a closed shop, knowing that information was power and not wanting to share either power or information with anyone outside his immediate circle.

With Manafort uninterested, I pushed our national security agenda and worked with Hope Hicks and campaign speechwriter Stephen Miller to get Trump's America First message framed into a major policy speech. We arranged for the speech to be hosted by the Center for the National Interest, which former president Richard M. Nixon had established to be a voice for "strategic realism." It was the perfect place for candidate Trump to give his first national security address. The speech laid out the intellectual framework for Trump's America First foreign policy. I reproduce the speech here not only for historical interest, but because its principles remain highly relevant.

Thank you for the opportunity to speak to you, and thank you to the Center for the National Interest for honoring me with this invitation.

I would like to talk today about how to develop a new foreign policy direction for our country—one that replaces randomness with purpose, ideology with strategy, and chaos with peace.

It is time to shake the rust off of America's foreign policy. It's time to invite new voices and new visions into the fold.

The direction I will outline today will also return us to a timeless principle. My foreign policy will always put the interests of the American people, and American security, above all else. That will be the foundation of every decision that I will make. America First will be the major and over-riding theme of my administration. But to chart our path forward, we must first briefly look back.

We have a lot to be proud of. In the 1940s we saved the world. The Greatest Generation beat back the Nazis and the Japanese Imperialists. Then we saved the world again, this time from totalitarian Communism. The Cold War lasted for decades, but we won. Democrats and Republicans working together got Mr. Gorbachev to heed the words of President Reagan when he said: "Tear down this wall." History will not forget what we did.

Unfortunately, after the Cold War, our foreign policy veered badly off course. We failed to develop a new vision for a new time. In fact, as time went on, our foreign policy began to make less and less sense. Logic was replaced with foolish-ness and arrogance, and this led to one foreign policy disaster after another. We went from mistakes in Iraq to Egypt to Libya, to President Obama's line in the sand in Syria. Each of these actions have helped to throw the region into chaos, and gave ISIS the space it needs to grow and prosper.

It all began with the dangerous idea that we could make Western democracies out of countries that had no experi-ence or interest in becoming a Western democracy. We tore up what institutions they had and then were surprised at what we unleashed. Civil war, religious fanaticism; thou-sands of American lives, and many trillions of dollars, were lost as a result. The vacuum was created that ISIS would fill. Iran, too, would rush in and fill the void, much to their unjust enrichment.

Our foreign policy is a complete and total disaster. No vision, no purpose, no direction, no strategy.

Today, I want to identify five main weaknesses in our foreign policy.

First, our resources are overextended.

President Obama has weakened our military by weakening our economy. He's crippled us with wasteful spending, massive debt, low growth, a huge trade deficit and open borders. Our manufacturing trade deficit with the world is now approaching $1 trillion a year. We're rebuilding other countries while weakening our own. Ending the theft of American jobs will give us the resources we need to rebuild our military and regain our financial independence and strength. I am the only person running for the presidency who understands this problem and knows how to fix it.

Second, our allies are not paying their fair share.

Our allies must contribute toward the financial, political, and human costs of our tremendous security burden. But many of them are simply not doing so. They look at the United States as weak and forgiving and feel no obligation to honor their agreements with us. In NATO, for instance, only 4 of 28 other member countries, besides America, are spending the minimum required 2 percent of GDP on defense.

We have spent trillions of dollars over time—on planes, missiles, ships, equipment—building up our military to provide a strong defense for Europe and Asia. The countries we are defending must pay for the cost of this defense—and, if not, the U.S. must be prepared to let these countries defend themselves. The whole world will be safer if our allies do their part to support our common defense and security. A Trump administration will lead a free world that is properly armed and funded.

Third, our friends are beginning to think they can't depend on us.

We've had a president who dislikes our friends and bows to our enemies. He negotiated a disastrous deal with Iran, and then we watched them ignore its terms, even before the ink was dry. Iran cannot be allowed to have a nuclear weapon and, under a Trump administration, will never be allowed to have a nuclear weapon. All of this without even mentioning the humiliation of the United States with Iran's treatment of our ten captured sailors.

In negotiation, you must be willing to walk. The Iran deal, like so many of our worst agreements, is the result of not being willing to leave the table. When the other side knows you're not going to walk, it becomes absolutely impossible to win. At the same time, your friends need to know that you will stick by the agreements that you have with them.

President Obama gutted our missile defense program, then abandoned our missile defense plans with Poland and the Czech Republic. He supported the ouster of a friendly regime in Egypt that had a longstanding peace treaty with Israel—and then helped bring the Muslim Brotherhood to power in its place.

Israel, our great friend and the one true democracy in the Middle East, has been snubbed and criticized by an administration that lacks moral clarity. Just a few days ago, Vice President Biden again criticized Israel—a force for justice and peace—for acting as an impediment to peace in the region. President Obama has not been a friend to Israel. He has treated Iran with tender love and care and made it a great power in the Middle East—all at the expense of Israel, our other allies in the region and, critically, the United States.

We've picked fights with our oldest friends, and now they're starting to look elsewhere for help.

Fourth, our rivals no longer respect us.

In fact, they are just as confused as our allies, but an even bigger problem is that they don't take us seriously anymore. When President Obama landed in Cuba on Air Force One, no leader was there to meet or greet him—perhaps an incident without precedent in the long and prestigious history of Air Force One. Then, amazingly, the same thing happened in Saudi Arabia—it's called no respect. Do you remember when the president made a long and expensive trip to Copenhagen, Denmark, to get the Olympics for our country, and, after this unprecedented effort, it was announced that the United States came in fourth place? He should have known the result before making such an embarrassing commitment.

The list of humiliations goes on and on. President Obama watches helplessly as North Korea increases its aggression and expands even further with its nuclear reach. Our president has allowed China to continue its economic assault on American jobs and wealth, refusing to enforce trade rules—or apply the leverage on China necessary to rein in North Korea. He has even allowed China to steal government secrets with cyberattacks and engage in industrial espionage against the United States and its companies.

We've let our rivals and challengers think they can get away with anything. If President Obama's goal had been to weaken America, he could not have done a better job.

Finally, America no longer has a clear understanding of our foreign policy goals.

Since the end of the Cold War and the breakup of the Soviet Union, we've lacked a coherent foreign policy. One day we're bombing Libya and getting rid of a dictator to foster democracy for civilians, the next day we are watching the same civilians suffer while that country falls apart.

We're a humanitarian nation. But the legacy of the Obama-Clinton interventions will be weakness, confusion, and disarray.

We have made the Middle East more unstable and chaotic than ever before. We left Christians subject to intense persecution and even genocide. Our actions in Iraq, Libya, and Syria have helped unleash ISIS. And we're in a war against radical Islam, but President Obama won't even name the enemy! Hillary Clinton also refuses to say the words "radical Islam," even as she pushes for a massive increase in refugees. After Secretary Clinton's failed intervention in Libya, Islamic terrorists in Benghazi took down our consulate and killed our ambassador and three brave Americans. Then, instead of taking charge that night, Hillary Clinton decided to go home and sleep! Incredible. Clinton blames it all on a video, an excuse that was a total lie. Our ambassador was murdered and our secretary of state misled the nation—and by the way, she was not awake to take that call at three o'clock in the morning. And now ISIS is making millions of dollars a week selling Libyan oil.

This will change when I am president.

To all our friends and allies, I say America is going to be strong again. America is going to be a reliable friend and ally again. We're going to finally have a coherent foreign policy based upon American interests, and the shared interests of our allies. We are getting out of the nation-building business, and instead focusing on creating stability in the world. Our moments of greatest strength came when politics ended at the water's edge. We need a new, rational American foreign policy, informed by the best minds and supported by both parties, as well as by our close allies. This is how we won the Cold War, and it's how we will win our new and future struggles.

First, we need a long-term plan to halt the spread and reach of radical Islam.

Containing the spread of radical Islam must be a major foreign policy goal of the United States. Events may require the use of military force. But it's also a philosophical struggle, like our long struggle in the Cold War. In this we're going to be working very closely with our allies in the Muslim world, all of which are at risk from radical Islamic violence.

We should work together with any nation in the region that is threatened by the rise of radical Islam. But this has to be a two-way street—they must also be good to us and remember us and all we are doing for them. The struggle against radical Islam also takes place in our homeland. There are scores of recent migrants inside our borders charged with terrorism. For every case known to the public, there are dozens more. We must stop importing extremism through senseless immigration policies. A pause for reassessment will help us to prevent the next San Bernardino or worse—all you have to do is look at the World Trade Center and September 11.

And then there's ISIS. I have a simple message for them. Their days are numbered. I won't tell them where and I won't tell them how. We must as, a nation, be more unpredictable. But they're going to be gone. And soon.

Second, we have to rebuild our military and our economy.

The Russians and Chinese have rapidly expanded their military capability, but look what's happened to us! Our nuclear weapons arsenal—our ultimate deterrent—has been allowed to atrophy and is desperately in need of modernization and renewal. Our active-duty armed forces have shrunk from 2 million in 1991 to about 1.3 million today. The navy has shrunk from over 500 ships to 272 ships during that time. The air force is about one-third smaller than 1991. Pilots are flying B-52s in combat missions today which are older than most people in this room.

And what are we doing about this? President Obama has proposed a 2017 defense budget that, in real dollars, cuts nearly 25 percent from what we were spending in 2011. Our military is depleted, and we're asking our generals and military leaders to worry about global warming. We will spend what we need to rebuild our military. It is the cheapest investment we can make. We will develop, build, and purchase the best equipment known to mankind. Our military dominance must be unquestioned.

But we will look for savings and spend our money wisely. In this time of mounting debt, not one dollar can be wasted. We are also going to have to change our trade, immigration, and economic policies to make our economy strong again—and to put Americans first again. This will ensure that our own workers, right here in America, get the jobs and higher pay that will grow our tax revenue and increase our economic might as a nation. We need to think smarter about areas where our technological superiority gives us an edge. This includes 3-D printing, artificial intelligence, and cyberwarfare.

A great country also takes care of its warriors. Our commitment to them is absolute. A Trump administration will give our service men and women the best equipment and support in the world when they serve, and the best care in the world when they return as veterans to civilian life.

Finally, we must develop a foreign policy based on American interests.

Businesses do not succeed when they lose sight of their core interests and neither do countries.

Look at what happened in the 1990s. Our embassies in Kenya and Tanzania were attacked and seventeen brave sailors were killed on the USS *Cole*. And what did we do? It seemed we put more effort into adding China to the World Trade Organization—which has been a disaster for the United States—than into stopping al Qaeda. We even had an opportunity to take out Osama Bin Laden, and didn't do it. And then, we got hit at the World Trade Center and the Pentagon, the worst attack on our country in its history.

Our foreign policy goals must be based on America's core national security interests, and the following will be my priorities. In the Middle East, our goals must be to defeat terrorists and promote regional stability, not radical change. We need to be clear-sighted about the groups that will never be anything other than enemies. And we must only be generous to those that prove they are our friends.

We desire to live peacefully and in friendship with Russia and China. We have serious differences with these two nations, and must regard them with open eyes. But we are not bound to be adversaries. We should seek common ground based on shared interests. Russia, for instance, has also seen the horror of Islamic terrorism.

I believe an easing of tensions and improved relations with Russia—from a position of strength—is possible. Common sense says this cycle of hostility must end. Some say the Russians won't be reasonable. I intend to find out. If we can't make a good deal for America, then we will quickly walk from the table.

Fixing our relations with China is another important step towards a prosperous century. China respects strength, and by letting them take advantage of us economically, we have lost all of their respect. We have a massive trade deficit with China, a deficit we must find a way, quickly, to balance. A strong and smart America is an America that will find a better friend in China. We can both benefit or we can both go our separate ways.

After I am elected president, I will also call for a summit with our NATO allies, and a separate summit with our Asian allies. In these summits, we will not only discuss a rebalancing of financial commitments, but take a fresh look at how we can adopt new strategies for tackling our common challenges. For instance, we will discuss how we can upgrade NATO's outdated mission and structure—grown out of the Cold War—to confront our shared challenges, including migration and Islamic terrorism.

I will not hesitate to deploy military force when there is no alternative. But if America fights, it must fight to win. I will never send our finest into battle unless necessary—and will only do so if we have a plan for victory. Our goal is peace and prosperity, not war and destruction. The best way to achieve those goals is through a disciplined, deliberate, and consistent foreign policy.

With President Obama and Secretary Clinton we've had the exact opposite: a reckless, rudderless, and aimless foreign policy—one that has blazed a path of destruction in its wake. After losing thousands of lives and spending trillions of dollars, we are in far worse shape now in the Middle East than ever before. I challenge anyone to explain the strategic foreign policy vision of Obama-Clinton—it has been a complete and total disaster.

I will also be prepared to deploy America's economic resources. Financial leverage and sanctions can be very persuasive—but we need to use them selectively and with determination. Our power will be used if others do not play by the rules. Our friends and enemies must know that if I draw a line in the sand, I will enforce it. However, unlike other candidates for the presidency, war and aggression will not be my first instinct. You cannot have a foreign policy without diplomacy. A superpower understands that caution and restraint are signs of strength.

Although not in government service, I was totally against the war in Iraq, saying for many years that it would desta-bilize the Middle East. Sadly, I was correct, and the biggest beneficiary was Iran, who is systematically taking over Iraq and gaining access to their rich oil reserves—something it has wanted to do for decades. And now, to top it all off, we have ISIS.

My goal is to establish a foreign policy that will endure for several generations. That is why I will also look for talented experts with new approaches, and practical ideas, rather than surrounding myself with those who have perfect resumes but very little to brag about except responsibility for a long history of failed policies and continued losses at war.

Finally, I will work with our allies to reinvigorate Western values and institutions. Instead of trying to spread "universal values" that not everyone shares, we should understand that strengthening and promoting Western civilization and its accomplishments will do more to inspire positive reforms around the world than military interventions.

These are my goals, as president.

I will seek a foreign policy that all Americans, whatever their party, can support, and which our friends and allies will respect and welcome. The world must know that we do not go abroad in search of enemies, that we are always happy when old enemies become friends, and when old friends become allies. To achieve these goals, Americans must have confidence in their country and its leadership again. Many Americans must wonder why our politicians seem more interested in defending the borders of foreign countries than their own. Americans must know that we are putting the American people first again. On trade, on immigration, on foreign policy—the jobs, incomes, and security of the American worker will always be my first priority. No country has ever prospered that failed to put its own interests first. Both our friends and enemies put their countries above ours and we, while being fair to them, must do the same.

We will no longer surrender this country, or its people, to the false song of globalism. The nation-state remains the true foundation for happiness and harmony. I am skeptical of international unions that tie us up and bring America down, and will never enter America into any agreement that reduces our ability to control our own affairs. NAFTA, as an example, has been a total disaster for the U.S. and has emptied our states of our manufacturing and our jobs. Never again. Only the reverse will happen. We will keep our jobs and bring in new ones. There will be consequences for companies that leave the U.S. only to exploit it later.

Under a Trump administration, no American citizen will ever again feel that their needs come second to the citizens of foreign countries. I will view the world through the clear lens of American interests. I will be America's greatest defender and most loyal champion. We will not apologize for becoming successful again, but will instead embrace the unique heritage that makes us who we are.

The world is most peaceful, and most prosperous, when America is strongest. America will continually play the role of peacemaker. We will always help to save lives and, indeed, humanity itself. But to play that role, we must make America strong again. We must make America respected again. And we must make America great again. If we do that, perhaps this century can be the most peaceful and prosperous the world has ever known. Thank you.

That was a great speech—and it is to Donald J. Trump's credit that he not only delivered a great speech, but once elected president, he lived up to it. The agenda laid out in that speech is the agenda he executed with remarkable success.

But first, of course, he had to get elected, and part of that strategy involved the selection of a vice president. Before Donald Trump decided on Mike Pence, he carefully considered other potential running mates. One of those Trump vetted as a possible vice presidential candidate was an old friend of mine, retired Lieutenant General Mike Flynn. Lt. Gen. Flynn had been director of the Defense Intelligence Agency before he was fired by President Obama. Flynn was a strong Trump supporter, and, personally, Trump liked him. A week after the Republican National Convention, Flynn and I met to discuss the campaign. Now that the Republican nomination was officially Trump's, and he was facing a former secretary of state in Hillary Clinton, defense and foreign policy were going to start playing a bigger role in the campaign. We resolved that when Flynn was not flying on Trump's gold-and-blue 757, "Trump Force One," I would be. We both knew Trump to be whip smart. Our job was to fill in any blanks he might have on defense and foreign policy details; it was never a matter of lectures, but of good, in-depth discussions.

As the Trump campaign now truly got under way, his primary national security advisers were Mike Flynn and me, with occasional assists from retired major general Bert Mizusawa and Jared Kushner, the president's son-in-law, who had a keen mind and an especial interest in advancing peace in the Middle East. Kushner was deeply involved in all aspects of the campaign. Trump valued his counsel.

In late August we also put together a new and exceptionally talented campaign team for the stretch run. We had a new campaign strategist in Steve Bannon, a former naval officer, successful businessman, and head of the Breitbart news website; a new campaign manager in political pollster Kellyanne Conway; and a new campaign operating officer in Dave Bossie, an experienced political activist whose job was to make sure everything ran smoothly.

The day after Manafort was removed, I sat down with Bannon, Bossie, and Kellyanne, and thought that we finally had the right team in place, people who understood Trump and fully supported his agenda. This was my first meeting with Steve Bannon, and we hit it off right away. It probably helped that our daughters were friends from their time together as cadets at the United States Military Academy at West Point. More important, I thought he had a great grasp of campaign and communications strategy and was as tough a fighter as Trump was. I also found myself impressed by Kellyanne and Dave Bossie. These were people unafraid of the odds against us, dedicated to the populist conservative cause, and energetic and imaginative in thinking of ways to advance the campaign. The campaign was now collaborative and very effective.

We set up a campaign war room on the fourteenth floor of Trump Tower to monitor media coverage of the day's events and to coordinate campaign activities. The data team, led by Brad Parscale, was up and running with an increased focus on making up ground in our "core four" must-win states of Florida, North Carolina, Iowa, and Ohio. Dave Bossie and Bannon had adjacent offices overlooking Fifth Avenue and were in constant motion. If we could hold the states won by Mitt Romney in 2012 and add those four, we would need only ten more Electoral College votes to win. We plotted six different paths to victory. The most direct was breaking through the "blue wall," the northern industrial states where a Republican presidential candidate had not won since 1988, but where we thought we could find potential Trump majorities, as Ronald Reagan had with the "Reagan Democrats" of the 1980s.

I put together lists of retired military and veterans' supporters, appeared on shows as a spokesman for candidate Trump, and briefed him in preparation for his debates. I found Trump to have an exceptional grasp of the issues. He clearly enjoyed debating them, asked in-depth questions, absorbed information quickly, was unafraid to challenge the dominant narrative in a room, and had an unerring instinct for getting to the heart of an issue.

Traveling with Trump gave me many opportunities to sit and talk with him; he was a genuinely fun guy to be around, with a wry sense of humor that the public seldom saw and with a sincere patriotism for which his enemies never gave him credit. I also witnessed how he was a prolific reader of newspapers and magazines and kept his own clip file of marked-up articles. He would take a highlighter to stories he thought were important from the *Wall Street Journal* and other newspapers, then tear the article out and drop it in the brown box that was constantly at his side. This was his own personal newspaper clipping service, and he kept himself very well informed on current events.

His opinions were those of a patriot who believed in American exceptionalism. He told me, "Obama-type globalism means that the United States shouldn't stand out among other nations but should blend seamlessly with the rest of the world. But there is no greater country than the United States, don't you think?" He thought that a choice between isolationism and globalism was a false choice put forward by the foreign policy establishment. The establishment sought to shore up support for its conventional wisdom by discrediting a commonsense national-interest approach to foreign affairs. What the American people wanted, Trump believed, was an America First policy, that, for instance, would stop wasting American dollars in the Middle East when we had more pressing needs closer to home—he pointed to inner-city schools and America's declining infrastructure as two examples. Far from disengaging from the world, he wanted America to lead. But he believed that leadership included getting other nations to do their part, including having our NATO allies spend more in their own defense, as they had agreed to do, only to then drag their feet about it. He also supported large increases in our own defense spending to make up for the deep defense cuts of the Obama administration that had undermined our military's readiness and modernization.

At some campaign events, Mike Flynn or I, or sometimes both of us, would give introductory remarks. Watching Donald Trump in action afterwards confirmed my belief that he would be a great president. People were thirsting for someone to talk *with* them and *for* them, not *to* them. Donald J. Trump was that someone. And they knew he was willing to fight for them. To Trump, every American was a person of importance. He didn't hide from the people. We'd go to a Holiday Inn Express, and he'd pose for a picture, sign an autograph, or simply talk with anyone who wished him well. Seeing the amazing size and enthusiasm of the

Trump crowds, recognizing that they saw Donald J. Trump as a beacon of hope for change, a spokesman for the common people of this country, I noted to myself, after one late campaign stop in Grand Junction, Colorado, in front of a massive overflow airport crowd, "No matter what happens, I am proud to be part of this effort, this change for America."

Late in the campaign, on a flight to New York from North Carolina, Trump mused, "Well, we gave it a great effort." It was the first and only time that I saw him almost resigning himself to the possibility of defeat. Kellyanne would hear nothing of it. She leaned in, pointed a finger in Trump's chest, and said loudly, "We are not going to lose, we are going to win. *We. Are. Going. To. Win.*"

I got up and moved to the front of the plane. I had figured with that outburst from her, it would be our last flight. Kellyanne followed me and winked. She and Bannon never showed any doubt about victory—and except for that one instance, Trump was equally confident, and indefatigable, rallying his supporters at event after event after event. But nearly everyone outside the campaign was predicting a crushing defeat for us. Still, the incredible, huge, enthusiastic crowds I saw that last week of the campaign convinced me we were going to win. They were like no political rallies I had ever seen or read about. Veterans, families, working people, happily waiting for hours to see and hear an unconventional candidate who promised to speak and fight for their interests.

Election Day broke bright and clear. The war room was up and running in Trump Tower. Turnout in rural areas was massive. Bannon texted me at 2:27 p.m., "Doing well... but pray."

The polls closed and the media, which had confidently predicted an overwhelming Hillary Clinton victory, began changing their tune. When the networks called Wisconsin for us, CNN pundit Jake Tapper said, "There goes the blue wall." It was more than that: it was game over.

CHAPTER SEVEN

Transitioning to America First

In the last month of the campaign, I split my time between working with the campaign staff in New York City and working with the transition office in Washington, D.C., which was headed by Chris Christie. My initial responsibilities on the transition team were focused on the Defense Department, but my portfolio quickly expanded to the Department of Veterans Affairs, the intelligence agencies, the Department of Homeland Security, and the National Security Council.

My team and I crafted agency action plans for our areas of responsibility and came up with small teams of vetted personnel who would work issues until the cabinet secretaries (whose confirmation hearings could take weeks) could appoint their own people to their departments.

Until the election, our transition team was very small. But winning changed everything. Walking into Trump Tower after the election was like walking into a different building. The Secret Service presence had dramatically increased. The side of Trump Tower facing Fifth Avenue was barricaded with New York City dump trucks filled with sand. That was expected. The new staffing at Trump Tower was not.

When I exited the elevator on the fourteenth floor two days after the election, I saw a beehive of activity, dozens of new faces, and my first thought was, "Who are all these people?"

I was talking with Dave Bossie in his office. His door opened and a woman stood there. Dave said, "Let me introduce Katie Walsh from the RNC. She is supporting Reince." I knew instantly that Reince Priebus, head of the Republican National Committee, was probably going to become White House chief of staff, and he was bringing in his team. The Republican establishment, which at first had tried to stop Trump from winning the nomination, and then had been tepid in its support, was about to take over the Trump presidency. I was furious. I told Dave Bossie and anyone else who would listen, including Jared Kushner and Ivanka Trump, and Jason Miller from the communications team, that we were going to lose what we had just won. The very people who—even after Trump had won the party's nomination had wanted him off the ticket—were going to claim that the administration was now theirs to operate, because they were the professionals.

The first meeting on senior personnel appointments was held on 11 November 2016. I was there with General Flynn, Jeff Sessions, Ivanka, Jared, Donald Trump, Jr., Eric Trump, and Bill Hagerty who had been head of the personnel team at the transition office. Steve Bannon had called Chris Christie away before the meeting, and the president-elect was not in attendance. Hagerty went down his list of key positions and recommendations.

I may have been a political rookie, but I knew a lot about personnel management decisions. I had done "hiring and firing" in both the military and business for more than thirty years, and I knew that putting the right team together would determine the success or failure of the administration.

I told the meeting, "We don't need a team of rivals; we need a cohesive team that will support the president-elect and his vision." I stressed the importance of loyalty to the president-elect, but it was clear that preference was being given to impressive resumes and shiny credentials,

Meeting with new Iraqi prime minister al-Kadhimi in the White House Cabinet Room. I am on the left side of the photo, sitting next to National Security Adviser Robert O'Brien. *Courtesy of White House photographer Shealah Craighead*

In the White House Situation Room in January 2020 with the National Security team, discussing the Iranian response to America's killing of Iranian terrorist mastermind General Qasem Soleimani. I am seated across from National Security Adviser Robert O'Brien and to the left of White House Chief of Staff Mulvaney. *Courtesy of White House photographer Shealah Craighead*

With Trump at Mar-a-Lago, February 2017. *Courtesy of White House photographer Shealah Craighead*

With Trump at a campaign discussion meeting at Trump Tower, September 2016. *Courtesy of the author*

At the November 2018 ASEAN Summit in Singapore with Vice President Pence, immediately before meeting with Russian president Vladimir Putin. *Courtesy of White House photographer D. Myles Cullen*

United Nations Security Council meeting on Venezuela with Vice President Pence, April 10, 2019. *Courtesy of the United Nations Photo Library*

At Mar-a-Lago with the president as he announces McMaster's appointment as national security adviser and mine as chief of staff to the National Security Council. *Courtesy of White House official photographer Shealah Craighead*

In the White House Oval Office with Army Delta Force "hero dog" Conan, who cornered ISIS leader al-Baghdadi in Syria. Baghdadi blew himself up. *Courtesy of the White House Photo Collection*

At Mar-a-Lago with the president and McMaster before a press conference. *Courtesy of White House photographer Shealah Craighead*

In the White House Cabinet Room going over global threats with the president, military leaders, the secretary of state, secretary of defense, and secretary of the treasury. General Milley, chairman of the Joint Chiefs of Staff, is leading the briefing. *Courtesy of the White House Photo Collection*

In the Oval Office with the president as he announces the U.S. Space Force, America's newest uniformed service. *Courtesy of White House photographer Shealah Craighead*

In the White House Situation Room with Larry Kudlow, chief economic adviser, for the G-7 video teleconference. *Courtesy of White House photographer Shealah Craighead*

November 2018 ASEAN
Summit in Singapore with
Vice President Pence and
National Security Adviser
Bolton. *Courtesy of the
ASEAN Summit*

Updating the vice
president before we go
into the Oval Office.
*Courtesy of White House
photographer D. Myles
Cullen*

The vice president's team in the Executive Office Building in the White House complex, coming from a discussion in the Vice President's Ceremonial Office. *Courtesy of White House photographer D. Myles Cullen*

A January 2021 discussion in the Oval Office on where to base new Space Force headquarters. Everyone is socially distanced. Trump selected Alabama. *Courtesy of White House Photo Collection*

Talking with the president and vice president on the White House colonnade and recommending that we strike Syria after the sarin nerve gas attack on civilians, April 2017. *Courtesy of White House photographer Shealah Craighead*

which I thought missed the point. Our goal was not—or should not have been—to reappoint prominent bureaucrats. Rather, our goal was—or should have been—to appoint people who believed, as Trump and his supporters did, that the government in Washington, D.C., needed a major course correction to put American interests, and the interests of America's working and middle classes, first. Or to put it in the Trump vernacular, we needed to "drain the swamp" of self-serving politicians, bureaucrats, and lobbyists who pushed a liberal, corporatist, internationalist agenda.

Most especially disturbing to me was that Bill Hagerty's personnel recommendations were overwhelmingly for people who had not been on the campaign. To my mind, it was obvious that people who sat out the campaign were far less likely to be eager, determined executors of the president's policies than those who had actively campaigned for him. That was just basic common sense. The Republican establishment wanted to control and tame the Trump administration before it even got started. One person who definitely understood this was Ivanka Trump; her own comments on personnel matters were always insightful.

What we really lost in those early days, weeks, and months was time. It took a long while for the right team to finally form in the Trump White House. No one on the personnel team had asked Trump about what sort of people he wanted in his cabinet and senior positions. And many of the appointments that were eventually made—including General Flynn as national security adviser, General Jim Mattis as secretary of defense, General John Kelly as chief of staff after Reince Priebus, Dan Coats as director of national intelligence, Mike Pompeo as director of central intelligence and then secretary of state—were not on the original personnel lists. The only one who was, who was named to a senior position, was Steve Mnuchin, who became secretary of the treasury.

The eventual director of presidential personnel, a critical hire, was Johnny DeStefano, a Reince Priebus selection from the Republican National Committee who told me that his preferred presidential candidate had been "any Republican." Not the answer I was hoping for. The man charged with staffing the White House was an establishment Republican who before he had worked at the RNC had worked for Republican congressman and Speaker of the House John Boehner.

The reason Chris Christie did not attend that first personnel meeting was that he was being removed as head of the transition team; he was replaced by a committee (of which he was a part). The new sixteen-person committee was chaired by the vice president–elect, and included Reince Priebus, Florida attorney general Pam Bondi, philanthropist Rebekah Mercer, Christie, and Mike Flynn.

Flynn was named Trump's national security adviser two weeks after the election. K.T. McFarland was named the deputy national security adviser just before Thanksgiving. Bannon, appointed chief strategist at the White House, asked me in late November what I wanted to do in the administration. I said, "Go home." He looked surprised. I told him, "Steve, if I had been appointed White House chief of staff, or nominated as secretary of defense, or national security adviser, or head of Veterans Affairs, I'd stay, because I could be a great assist to the president in what I believe will be a tough governing environment. But those positions are all taken—and I'm fine with that. I don't want a job just for the sake of having a job. I don't want to be buried in some department just so I can say I work for the administration. We helped get the right guy elected president—and that's enough for me. I intend to go back into the business world and private life."

The next day, as I was getting ready to leave Trump Tower for D.C., Bannon caught me and said, "I know what they're going to ask you to do."

"Who is *they*?"

"*They* is me."

He added that he and Priebus had agreed that I should serve as chief of staff to the National Security Council. The head of the NSC is the national security adviser, the president's principal counselor on national security issues—and that would be my old friend, General Mike Flynn. Bannon pressed, "We want you in the White House."

I still wasn't sure, but I saw Flynn and McFarland sitting together in a conference room. I dropped in on them and Flynn said, "Congratulations. You're being announced as the NSC chief of staff. Monica Crowley will be our spokesperson."

Well, then, I guess it was a done deal.

Monica and I were announced as NSC appointments later that day.

But I still wasn't sure about the idea.

That Sunday, after Mass, I got a call from Steve Bannon. I told him I wasn't sure I was the right person for the chief of staff job. What I didn't say, but was thinking, was that I wasn't sure Mike Flynn and K.T. McFarland were the right appointments either. Before I got halfway through my thought, Bannon cut me off, "Wait, brother. I want you there. Reince and I have divided some responsibilities. National security matters will be my concern. I'm not sure about Mike and I don't have confidence in K.T. She has been out of the business too long. She wasn't on the campaign. I don't know what she really thinks. I need you there. You can provide balance. If necessary, you can be a buffer between them and the president."

I wondered how Flynn and McFarland had been appointed in the first place if Bannon wasn't confident in them. But I said, "Okay, I understand," because I deeply wanted President Trump to be successful, and if my taking the position helped in some way, I'd do it.

On Monday, I called Mike Flynn and asked how he wanted to organize the NSC team. We could do it by region (Russia, Middle East, China), function (counter-terrorism, nuclear proliferation, health), or some other combination. Mike said he hadn't thought about organization just yet. I told him that was fine, I'd develop some options, but that he should talk with Trump to find out what sort of NSC he wanted, because ultimately it was the president's staff, not his.

Obama's NSC had almost three hundred people in it. Flynn thought that was an appropriate staffing level. I thought it was way too big, bound to be inefficient, and at that size was unlikely to be staffed by people dedicated to the Trump agenda. If we had to fill three hundred positions, we'd get a lot of bureaucratic retreads.

After Christmas, Tom Bossert, who had served in the George W. Bush administration, was named assistant to the president for homeland security and counter-terrorism, a position that the transition team in New York said would be "equal in status to Flynn." If that were true, it showed a shocking lack of confidence in Flynn, and sent a warning to me that Flynn would not be fully in charge of the NSC.

A week later I met with Tom Bossert. I showed him an organizational chart that had General Flynn at the top of the NSC with K.T. McFarland as his sole deputy. Bossert, as an assistant to the president, would have within his portfolio homeland security and anti-terrorism. I told him that I chose the designation anti-terrorism for a reason. It implied stateside responsibilities. Counter-terrorism implied involvement in actions overseas, which were the purview of the national security adviser. Bossert demanded the counter-terrorism portfolio, and when I pushed back, he slammed his hand on the table and said, "That's the way it needs to be!"

I called Flynn and told him that unless he reined Bossert in, unless he asserted his authority, the responsibility for counter-terrorism matters would be split, dangerously I thought, between him and another assistant to the president. An assistant to the president generally has "walk in" privileges to the Oval Office. I told Flynn that if Bossert had such access when it came to counter-terrorism, it would certainly undercut his authority and that of the National Security Council, and lead to confusion when it came to policy and communication. Neither he nor K.T. seemed concerned. But I think some of the alleged "chaos" in the early days of the Trump administration confirmed my worries; not everyone in the administration was on the same page when it came to the president's policies and his message. Flynn chose not to weigh in on Bossert's "title," and Bossert got the counter-terrorism portfolio he wanted. It would stay that way until John Bolton became the president's national security adviser, when Bossert was removed and the title was eliminated. Bolton knew and understood more about bureaucratic politics than Flynn did.

As the transition proceeded, all the work I had done with the transition team, all the policy preparation for the first one hundred days of the administration, all the lists of landing teams who could help cabinet secretaries get started on their work, proved to be for naught. A week before the inauguration, I was told to collect all the plans and lists and destroy them. We were to do nothing to guide the cabinet secretaries or their departments. It was to be a huge unforced error on our part.

I was stunned. The only consolation I had was that we had our NSC team ready to go, and I felt it was a good one, for the most part. Suzy George, Obama's executive secretary of the NSC, proved to be immensely helpful and incredibly gracious with her time. Working together, I thought we had the NSC staff set up, as best we could, for long-term success in being supportive to the president. Of course, what we didn't know was that Mike Flynn's run as national security adviser would last fewer than thirty days.

■ ■ ■

My goal in assembling the National Security Council staff was to have in place people who shared the president's basic foreign policy principles. Those principles were easily explained. Finding people who honestly and fully shared them was not—at least not among experienced foreign policy bureaucrats for whom liberal internationalism was unquestionable orthodoxy.

Once, when I was sitting across from Trump on a campaign flight, he said to me, "Saving the world is noble. But it shouldn't be done solely at our expense. Our allies need to pull their weight. The primary objective of American foreign policy should be the promotion of American self-interest." There it was: America First. Every decision I saw the president make was based on that prescription: what would best serve American interests. When people came to him with proposed international agreements or diplomatic initiatives, his first question was always "What's in it for the United States?" When he met with foreign leaders, he was not afraid to say, "Why are we subsidizing you?" or "Why are your tariffs higher on our goods?" or "Why aren't you supporting American policy on China or Iran or Israel?" Many foreign leaders were caught short by this approach. They were unused to an American president boldly promoting American interests rather than seeking to go along with a presumed international consensus.

Trump was a foreign policy and economic realist. He believed in economic and foreign policy nationalism. He was deeply opposed to expending American blood and treasure unless it was necessary; to do otherwise, he thought, was a betrayal of the American people—most especially our soldiers—and a path to civilizational decline. People greatly underestimate Trump's strategic vision and intelligence. If you want to get a good grasp of how Trump thinks, read Paul Kennedy's *The Rise and Fall of the Great Powers*. Kennedy writes about the interaction of economics and strategy, and how great powers often overextend their strategic and economic reach, leading to decline and fall. Trump had a very similar view, which is why he thought of diplomacy as a transactional business. It was not about—or should not be about—pursuing the agenda of liberal internationalism. Instead, American diplomats should always be looking to advance American interests. Trump was the only viable candidate of either party to call for ending American involvement in wars that brought no benefit to the American people. On the campaign trail, Trump often talked about "taking the oil" of hostile regimes in the Middle East or Near East. He meant two things by this: one, he thought it was outrageous that American blood should be shed in places like Iraq, only to see Chinese oil companies (among others) profit; and two, he wanted to prevent hostile countries (like Iran) or terrorist groups (like ISIS) from selling oil on the black market. In short, he wanted to weaken our enemies; he wanted our allies to strengthen themselves; and most of all, he wanted America to defend its own interests. To remain the preeminent leader in the world, America needed the world's strongest economy and strongest military. He was determined to deliver both. As he said in his acceptance speech at the 2016 Republican convention: "Our plan will put America first. Americanism, not globalism, will be our credo. As long as we are led by politicians who will not put America first, then we can be assured that other nations will not treat America with respect....The American people will come first once again....I am your voice."

Trump's vision had been so well articulated in his speeches and books—for those with ears to hear and eyes to see—that it might have been easy to assume that those taking positions in his administration would push those policies. But the pull of conventional thinking, the long-standing Washington liberal consensus, was too much for many. We had many people who wanted administration jobs for the sake of those jobs. Many were not open about their disagreements with the president. That, needless to say, became a source of trouble and greatly hindered the administration's effectiveness, as we were constantly battling not just congressional Democrats, the media, and never-Trump Republicans, but doubters within our own ranks.

Sun Tzu wrote, "Know the enemy and know yourself; in a hundred battles you will never be in peril. When you are ignorant of the enemy, but know yourself, your chances of winning or losing are equal. If ignorant of both your enemy and yourself, you are certain in every battle to be in peril." Our problem was that we did not always know who our enemies were; in some cases, they were our own political appointees.

CHAPTER EIGHT

Out Like Flynn

On Inauguration Day, I was the first staffer to enter the West Wing of the White House. Bannon had wanted to have a small NSC team on the ground during the transition of government in the unlikely event something went wrong. Thankfully, nothing did.

President Obama's administration officially ended at noon, 20 January 2017. At exactly 12:01 (I looked at my watch) we were allowed in the West Wing, as President Trump was sworn in. Members of the White House Military Office led us to the Roosevelt Room on the second floor, just feet away from the Oval Office. The Roosevelt Room, used mostly as a conference room, was named by President Nixon in 1969 to honor Theodore Roosevelt and Franklin Delano Roosevelt, both of whom are depicted in large oil paintings. Theodore Roosevelt is portrayed on horseback, in his Rough Rider uniform. The painting of him hangs over the room's fireplace and is framed by his Medal of Honor and Nobel Peace Prize. The portrait of Franklin Roosevelt shows him working at his desk. The flags of the military services are present (with their battle streamers), along with an American flag, and the colors of the president and vice president. I could not help but feel that I was surrounded by history, and that the ghosts of earlier generations were watching to ensure I did my duty.

Once we had our blue badges that gave us official access to the West Wing and through U.S. Secret Service checkpoints, we were able to walk around and get settled. I walked to my office, which was on the ground floor of the West Wing, or the "lower suite." I called my office "the closet." It was small, but it was in the West Wing—and in the White House it's all about location, location, location.

The West Wing itself is small, and after a couple of weeks, everyone knows everyone else, at least by sight. Every important room in the West Wing is within two minutes' walk, and that includes the majestic Oval Office of the president.

The inauguration was on Friday. On Monday we had our first (and inconsequential) meeting with the new White House chief of staff, Reince Priebus. After the meeting, I crossed over into Steve Bannon's office. Steve's office was smaller and less ornate than Reince's. It had no fireplace or "corner office" look. But what really set it apart was that Bannon had covered his walls with butcher paper. On this paper he wrote, using a black Sharpie, his recommended strategic goals for the first one hundred days of the administration. Next to each goal was a square waiting for a checkmark that would show it had been achieved. As the days went by, Bannon scribbled out new tasks and goals. West Wing standard décor, it was not. Steve thought strategically and did not care about appearances or looks. I confess, he always struck me as a bit of a mad scientist; this just helped to confirm it. During the campaign there were times when he was on his two cell phones simultaneously and carrying on a coherent conversation with me.

The differences between Priebus and Bannon were striking, and not just in appearance. Bannon was a populist; Priebus a "traditional" Republican. I liked Steve's approach to life and politics. He understood and respected the president's base. He was more concerned about the people in Washington, Kansas, than the politicians in Washington, D.C. Like Trump, he believed in action—getting things done, now.

It quickly became apparent that the administration was divided into tribes. Reince led the traditional Republican tribe. He was our link to the RNC and the Republican congressional leadership. Bannon led the populist tribe—the tribe that best represented the president's beliefs. And then there was the internationalist tribe, led by Gary Cohn, director of the National Economic Council, and a Democrat, who represented our link to Wall Street, big business, and any Democrats who were willing to deal with us.

At the beginning, the tribes were all reasonably friendly to each other. But as former secretary of defense Robert Gates once said, "Being friendly does not make you friends." The truce between the tribes would not last long.

At the closeout for our first full day in the West Wing, K.T. McFarland, Mike Flynn, and I were sitting with our executive assistants in Mike's office. The door opened suddenly, and in walked the president carrying a picture of Abraham Lincoln. He announced, "Look what I found." I silently hoped it had not come off one of the West Wing walls. He reassured us that he had found it in a closet. He was in a great mood.

We told him we were discussing how to achieve his goal of withdrawing our troops from Afghanistan and ending America's longest war. He nodded his head, started out of the office, then turned and said, "On Afghanistan: end that thing." He wanted our troops home and the money saved from overseas deployments used to restore America's own infrastructure. Strategically, he wanted the United States to pivot from focusing on Afghanistan to the bigger challenges of the Pacific region, including North Korea and its nuclear weapons program, and the growing threat from China. Four years later, our senior national security and foreign policy leadership had failed him on that.

The next morning, I returned to Mike Flynn's spacious corner office in the West Wing. The national security adviser's office is on the same floor as the Oval Office, the vice president's office, and the chief of staff's office. It has been that way since the days of Henry Kissinger.

(He had once been in the same office I was in, but wanted to be closer to the president.)

Mike was behind closed doors, so I asked the executive officer who was with him. He said, "The FBI," and, almost simultaneously, the door opened and two FBI agents walked out. I would later recognize one of them as the infamous Peter Strzok. After they had gone, I asked Mike what that was all about.

He said, "Just some transition things. Nothing to worry about."

"I should have been in here with you. If anyone knew what we did in the transition it was me."

"Really, it was nothing."

"Maybe so, but it doesn't seem right that they should be here on our second workday. Next time, you should have the NSC lawyer with you."

Months later, when I was questioned for almost five hours by Special Counsel Robert Mueller's team, I found that Flynn's discussions with the FBI were far more consequential than I had imagined.

By the middle of this first week, the secretary of defense, retired general Jim Mattis, and the chairman of the Joint Chiefs, General Joe Dunford, were coming over to brief the president and vice president on a military operation and gain their approval. What I did not know until shortly before the meeting was that the operation had been planned during the waning days of the Obama administration and not executed. This would be an operational briefing, where Trump would be asked to make an immediate decision with near-term consequences, a decision that would put American troops in harm's way.

I assumed the briefing would take place in the Situation Room, which is a secure conference room in the West Wing with seating for thirty-four people and global electronic connections. It is staffed twenty-four hours a day, seven days a week by eight- to ten-person teams. The watch officers can connect the president to anyone in a matter of minutes.

But just as he had been an unconventional candidate, so the president proved to be an unconventional president. Melania and Barron had yet to arrive from New York City, and he wanted a relaxed environment for our discussions. He wanted to do the briefing over dinner at the residence, with the vice president and CIA director Mike Pompeo and others in attendance.

That evening I joined Mike Flynn and Reince Priebus and the three of us walked over together to the residence. We met the vice president in the state dining room. Jared Kushner, Steve Bannon, and Mike Pompeo were already there. It was my first dinner in the White House—and in the state dining room no less. It was a large venue for a small dinner, let alone a briefing. Generals Mattis and Dunford came in together and the president joined us shortly thereafter. After dinner, the tables were cleared and the support staff left the room. The discussion centered on a military operation Generals Mattis and Dunford recommended we execute in Yemen. Not in two months or two weeks, but in *two days*. Something did not feel right. I sat at the other end of the table and to the left of Vice President Pence. The generals had charts for the president to look at, but we couldn't see them. We listened intently as they discussed a combined Emirati/U.S. raid by our special operators against an al Qaeda target in Yemen. It was a "sensitive site exploitation" mission. In plain speak, it was a military raid to gather information.

Planned during the Obama administration, the military had been waiting for optimum conditions (including a moonless night) to execute the plan. With advanced night-vision technology, our military enjoys a tremendous advantage in night operations. As Special Operations forces like to say, "We own the night."

With the change in administration, the mission needed the new commander in chief's approval. The mission did not seem overly complicated. A quick hit, in and out. The president obviously trusted the two four-star generals—one retired (Mattis), one active (Dunford)—doing the briefing; and he trusted his retired three-star general national security adviser, Mike Flynn, who seemed supportive of the plan. I trusted Mattis and Dunford too, and I had no reason to doubt Mike Flynn. But what I did doubt was the necessity of the operation. I kept asking myself, "If Obama had put off the decision to execute this plan, why can't we wait as well?" The mission did not involve American hostages. There was no imminent threat to the United States. The target was not fleeing anywhere. And we, as a national security team, were just finding our footing. Surely this operation was not so pressing that we needed to do it in the first week of the president's administration. I regret to say that I kept my counsel to myself. It would be the last time I would ever do that in the White House. We owed it to "them," those in the field, to give the president our very best counsel.

Later, I told Mike that he should have required Mattis to defend the mission, not just brief it. I felt the new secretary of defense had rolled him. Mike was the national security adviser to the president; Mattis was not. Multiple eyes needed to be on those missions. Not for micromanagement reasons, but to ensure that the president received a full range of views and analysis from our National Security Council team. The president was not shy about making hard decisions, far from it, but he deserved our best counsel. He would be putting American troops in harm's way, and we owed it to those troops to give the commander in chief all the relevant information and advice that we had to inform his decision. But this operation had been presented to us more or less as a *fait accompli* to which the president merely had to say yes—and clearly was expected to say yes.

As Mattis and Dunford were finishing up, I wrote a quick note to the vice president. I had a question I thought he should ask. I knew if he asked it, it would carry more weight than if I did. "Secretary Mattis, what is your risk assessment?"

"Very low. Almost negligible."

In my experience, no military operation is ever low risk. As the saying goes, the enemy always gets a vote.

The president approved the raid.

Two nights later, the assault went in.

It was not low risk. The enemy voted. A steep price would be paid—as we would soon find out.

■ ■ ■

After the briefing, the president took us on a personal tour of the residence. Free from family obligations until his wife and son arrived, he spent a lot of time showing us around. He loved the residence and proved to be a first-rate tour guide.

Making our farewell to the president, we walked through the colonnade connecting the residence with the West Wing.

General Dunford said, "He trusts us. We can't screw this up."

I said, "I know. That's my fear. He trusts you too much."

Humans make mistakes, and generals are human.

■ ■ ■

The raid went down on the night of 29 January 2017. There was a fight. A Navy SEAL, Chief Petty Officer William "Ryan" Owens, was killed by enemy rifle fire and several others were wounded. Civilians were killed, including an eight-year-old Yemeni child. A Special Operations—MV-22 Osprey aircraft was lost as well. The friction of war had kicked in. The risk was not negligible.

When I took the call from the Situation Room on the results of the mission, we were told it was a success. The Joint Staff told us they were able to capture and exploit "sensitive al Qaeda material." In English: we recovered documents, cell phones, and computers. They were investigating what happened during the mission with the loss of life and aircraft.

The very personal human part came next. The remains of Navy SEAL Owens arrived home on 1 February 2017, at Dover Air Force Base. His arrival home was a solemn ceremony that honored his sacrifice. The military protocol is to conduct a "dignified transfer." On arrival, those who have made the ultimate sacrifice in the course of duty are to be respected and honored. Military escorts carry the worldly remains out of the transport aircraft to a transfer vehicle, which takes them to the mortuary center. It is, in its simplicity, a moving ceremony. Senior officials attend to pay their respects and honor those who gave their all. The president and his oldest daughter, Ivanka, attended Ryan's ceremony.

Just over a week after he assumed his constitutional role as commander in chief, President Trump was paying tribute to a service member he had sent into battle. He honored that hero's sacrifice by being present, as did Ivanka. General Mattis was not among them. He later released a written statement of sympathy.

These are understandably difficult ceremonies. The families of the fallen are often emotional. Ryan's father, Bill, did not want to meet the president. He was not convinced the raid had been worth Ryan's life. He was probably thinking, as I had, that there was no need for the president, in his first week in office, to rush into a military operation. Acknowledging the emotion and the loss of a loved one far from home, the president said simply, "There is nothing worse." It was obvious to me that President Trump felt the full weight of the commander in chief's responsibility.

Landing in Marine One later in the day on the South Lawn, I talked with Ivanka after she reentered the West Wing. She admitted how hard the ceremony had been, and how moved her father was. After the Yemeni raid, the president never again took the counsel of his generals without deep questioning. America First, in his mind, very much included not taking unnecessary risks with the lives of our service members. As would prove true in Afghanistan, that didn't mean he would override the advice of his generals, but he always demanded thoroughly convincing arguments. I would constantly reinforce his instinct that generals are not always right.

Every administration creates a concise National Security Memorandum, approved and signed by the president. Our first was rolled out one week after the inauguration. The president wanted his first presidential memorandum to be on "Rebuilding the Armed Forces." The second, which we released the next day, was a memorandum I had written during the transition on how we intended to organize the National Security

Council. Boring for most people—but not to the Washington press corps, which completely ignored the first memorandum to focus on one aspect of the second. That aspect was that the chief strategist in the White House, Steve Bannon, would be a regular invited attendee at NSC meetings. Choosing who attends NSC meetings is a prerogative of the president. It is his National Security Council. Listening to the press reports, you would have thought we were trying to overthrow the Republic. The press regarded Bannon as a political dark prince.

Me? I was fine with his attendance. The great military theorist Carl von Clausewitz wrote that war is a continuation of politics by other means. To me politics is war by another name. Bannon was a legitimate political strategist, reflected the president's own views on foreign policy, and, as a former naval officer, knew something about defense and national security. I was much more interested in hearing what he had to say at NSC meetings than I was in listening to press complaints about his attendance. A significant part of the mainstream media was engaged in a constant propaganda war against us, and there was no reason why our organizational and policy decisions should have been dictated by a hostile press.

I told Mike Flynn not to worry about the media, to double down on our commitment to the NSC organizational memorandum, and to reassure President Trump that he would get the NSC organization he wanted. But Flynn was nervous about the negative press reports. He didn't like the aspersions being cast upon the NSC—that we had politicized it and made it less professional (or less bound by conventional thinking) by including Bannon. Mike pulled the memo, and Bannon's seat at the NSC table would soon be removed.

Late in the afternoon on Monday, 13 February 2017, I was in Mike's office with K.T. McFarland, talking about the events of the day and our progress in coming up with plans to execute the president's top foreign policy and defense priorities, which included defeating ISIS and withdrawing from Afghanistan. Mike appeared distracted. He had been that way for a week. I assumed it was the long hours we were putting in. We came to work when it was dark, left when it was dark, and Mike was in the Oval Office constantly. The president could be a tough and exacting taskmaster. The stress of trying to achieve his goals in the teeth of establishment opposition was understandable. But this seemed to go beyond that. I sensed something was wrong.

I asked Mike, "Is everything okay? Is there something K.T. and I need to know?"

Mike said, "No, everything is fine."

A little later, we were in the Oval Office waiting for the swearing-in of Steve Mnuchin as secretary of the treasury. I was standing next to K.T. and Mike was to her left. I noticed Reince Priebus in the doorway signaling for Mike. I gave Mike a nudge and he left with Reince. I thought nothing of it and continued to talk with K.T. In less than ten minutes, Reince was back at the Oval entrance door and this time he signaled for me to come out. He said we needed to go down to my office.

We went in. Reince shut the door and told me that Mike had been asked to resign. I was going to be the acting national security adviser.

"Why's Mike resigning?"

"I'll explain later."

"Why not elevate K.T.?"

"Because we all have full confidence in you."

I assumed "we" meant the president, the vice president, Reince, and Bannon.

He told me to stay in the office until he came back. He implied that Mike was still in the complex, and he wanted no interaction between us.

I confess that after a short interval, I snuck out to the navy mess around the corner from my office and got a chicken sandwich—and felt strangely guilty about it.

Reince returned to my office in about an hour and said Mike had departed the complex. He added that Mike had been removed, ultimately, because he had lied to Vice President Pence. Mike had told him that he had not talked to the Russian ambassador Sergey Kislyak during the transition about lifting Obama-era sanctions when, in fact, he had.

Vice President Pence had been asked on a Sunday news show about any such conversations between administration officials and the Russians. He denied any contact, based on what Flynn had told him. Not good.

Still, I looked at Reince in near disbelief. It was one thing for Flynn to have lied—that was unmistakably, undoubtedly wrong. But as for talking with the Russians—of course we had talked to the Russians! We had talked to the Spanish and the Germans too during the transition. So what? We were the transitioning government; that's what incoming administrations do. It's about making introductions and establishing contacts for both continuity and change.

The FBI visit to Flynn two weeks earlier now loomed large in my mind. That, and the fact that Flynn had not told Reince, the White House counsel, the president, or the vice president about it until much later. That was a monumental error, and I could only assume that Flynn had lied to Pence because he had been spooked by that FBI visit. I thought, too, about Bannon's comment during the transition that he wasn't convinced that Flynn was the right person to be national security adviser or that K.T. McFarland was the right deputy. Perhaps he thought they were too naïve about the bureaucratic battles to come.

Late that night I met with Bannon and Reince. Reince asked if I would like to be appointed as the national security adviser—not just in an acting capacity. I told him of course I would, but that was up to the president. I added that they did Trump no favors unless they found someone who was completely compatible with him in terms of policy, personality, and ability to take the heat. After what had happened with Mike, they had to get this one right. Mike had violated the trust of both the president and the vice president; they needed to find someone who could regain that trust.

The week proved to be frenetic. The press went crazy as usual, but behind the scenes there was intense lobbying among several candidates to be Flynn's replacement. I was in the room when the president conducted a phone interview with Dave Petraeus, who had a list of "demands." That was the end of his candidacy. You do not bargain with the president of the United States, especially when his name is Donald Trump.

It was obvious to me that certain people were putting markers down. When retired navy vice admiral Bob Harward's name surfaced, I suspected he was being pushed by Secretary of Defense Jim Mattis. No one on the Trump team knew him and he had not been part of the campaign, but he had worked with Mattis in the past. I knew Bob, and, in fact, I had met with him in my office in the West Wing just a week before. Bob is a genuinely good man who had an exceptional navy career in the SEALs. He had just lined up a great civilian position that paid a lot of money, that would give his family some stability, and that would allow him to buy his dream house in southern California. I was certain he was not interested in a government job.

But over the course of a week, Bob went from being the dark horse candidate that no one knew to becoming the lead candidate that everyone liked. It was then that K.T. McFarland made a huge mistake. She reached out to Bob and lobbied to keep her position if he were selected. She told no one about it. Bob did. When Bob declined the position, he told the president and Reince about how K.T. had lobbied him. It was clear to the president and everyone else that she had tried to retain her position by bad-mouthing everyone else. As it was relayed to me, "She threw everyone under the bus." The president was, to put it mildly, not happy...not happy at all.

The search for a new national security adviser continued. A group of us were heading to Mar-a-Lago for the weekend, and before departing the White House the president tweeted, "General Keith Kellogg, who I have known for a long time, is very much in play for NSA—as are three others." I did not know it then, but the "three others" would meet with us in Florida over the weekend.

Boarding Air Force One on Friday, I joined Reince and Steve Bannon as we jetted towards what we called the southern White House. Settling into a Mar-a-Lago poolside room overlooking the ocean, it felt surreal. That evening at dinner, the patio dining area was packed, and the president and First Lady were greeted like rock stars. As primary staff, we sat a table away. I am sure it drove the Secret Service nuts, but, over coffee, it was fun to watch people jockeying to see the president.

Saturday proved to be quiet. I updated the president on a couple of international issues but, for the most part, it was a routine Saturday. He played some golf and we all relaxed. It felt good to be away from D.C.

Later that day, talking with Reince, he told me that three people were coming to interview with the president: John Bolton, army lieutenant general Bob Caslen, and army lieutenant general H.R. McMaster.

I told Reince (and Bannon later) that I thought this was idiotic. We were wasting the president's time and not serving him well by having him sit down with three men who had not been on the campaign, had no obvious connection to the president's policies, and had been vetted in one day. Everyone knew Bolton—and knew that his preference for a heavily interventionist foreign policy was antithetical to the president's agenda; his only recommendation was that he was a long-standing Republican foreign policy functionary. I was the only one who knew Lt. Gens. Caslen and McMaster. They were active-duty army generals who did not know the president and had no knowledge of politics, with one admitting he was totally apolitical and had never even voted. In Washington, D.C., no one gets to be apolitical. Every national security decision is guided by administration policy and strategy, which means politics. But for this appointment, Reince and Bannon seemed far less interested in finding someone whose views and personality were compatible with the president than they were with moving quickly to put Flynn behind them. They thought they could appease the media critics by giving them a name they might respect. Bob Caslen, whom I had known for years, was the superintendent of the U.S. Military Academy at West Point. Lt. Gen. McMaster held a PhD in American history from the University of North Carolina at Chapel Hill. Bolton was an experienced Washington hand, if nothing else. He had held positions in the Reagan administration and both Bush administrations and been an adviser to Republican presidential candidate Mitt Romney in 2012. He was the choice of the Republican establishment—the establishment that Donald Trump had overturned.

Early Monday morning I received a call from the Situation Room. The Russian ambassador to the United Nations, Vitaly Churkin, had just died from a heart attack in New York City.

I went to alert the president so he would not be caught short if someone asked him about it. Walking into the ornate lobby of Mar-a-Lago, with its always stunning display of red or yellow roses, I saw the president sitting with H.R. McMaster, Priebus, and Bannon. After acknowledgments, I told the president about Churkin. The president said, "Sit down with us." It was clear he was offering McMaster the position as national security adviser. I shot a look at Bannon that probably said it all and asked if he and I could excuse ourselves for a minute. We went to the small bar off the lobby. Moving into the bar area, I was profanely blunt. I was livid. They had vetted a guy in under twenty-four hours, a guy not associated politically with the president, who knew next to nothing about him. I was even angrier that they hadn't bothered to ask for my opinion before inviting him for an interview. I said, "You're setting the president up for failure. You are not looking out for him. This is pure expediency."

Bannon had no response because the die was cast. We went back into the lobby. The president was closing with McMaster and said, "I would like you to be in uniform when I make the announcement." The deal was done.

The president looked at me and said, "You can work with H.R., right?"

I dodged. I said, "Mr. President, let me talk with H.R. to make sure we are both okay with it."

McMaster and I walked outside. I told him I was not sure this arrangement would work. I had been with the president and knew his style. I knew the president was smart, and I knew McMaster was smart too. But he tended to lecture people. That style would not work well with the president. He asked difficult questions. He wanted direct answers. He liked give and take.

McMaster said let's try it for a while and see if it works out. I went back to my room and got ready to fly home after the press announcement. In my gut, I knew there would be friction. As a campaign veteran, I believed that advancing the president's agenda was paramount. For me, it was damn near a crusade. Our personalities, McMaster's and mine, were significantly different, as was how we viewed the job. I did not see how this would end well for anyone.

Going back to the Mar-a-Lago lobby before the press conference, the president called me into the side bar. Bannon must have talked to him. He looked at me and said directly, "Are you okay with this?" I delayed and he picked up on the pause. The president said, "If you are not with me on this, I don't want you to be part of the press announcement."

After another long pause, I said, "I'm in."

He said, "Okay, I will introduce McMaster, make a few comments, say you are the chief of staff, and we will be done."

Shortly after the press conference, we boarded Air Force One to head back to Washington. The Flynn NSC was in the past. His replacement was someone who was definitely "book smart," but I did not feel good about the future.

CHAPTER NINE

Restarting at the National Security Council

I t felt like we were back at day one. McMaster told me he was "apolitical" and wanted to run an apolitical National Security Council. There is no doubting McMaster's intelligence, but an apolitical National Security Council was an impossibility. Still, that was part of his decision to serve as national security adviser while remaining an active army general.

His lack of political savvy would, I thought, be a handicap in working with the president. Donald J. Trump is quick witted, with incredible instincts. While most people play political checkers, he plays three-dimensional political chess, and if, as an adviser, you can't keep up with his reasoning, you can't serve him well. Someone who was not in sync with Trump's thinking would have a hard time in an already hard job.

That's not to say that President Trump's goals and beliefs were overly complicated. They weren't. He knew what he wanted and his beliefs were an open book. He had written about them or spoken about them at length. All politicians change their positions from time to time, but Trump had been remarkably consistent with his nationalist, patriotic, populist agenda. To me, there were no policy surprises with President Donald J. Trump.

I believed our job at the National Security Council was to coordinate and guide the president's directives through the agencies and departments. And this was the problem. That was not McMaster's view. He did not fully embrace what President Trump wanted to accomplish, from applying pressure on our NATO allies to increase their contributions to the alliance to ending America's longest war and withdrawing American troops from Afghanistan. Instead, he thought it was his job to school the president, guide him, and convince him to pursue more conventional and traditional courses of action. That was never going to work. Part of being successful is understanding your boss. McMaster didn't know his.

I was fortunate to see Donald J. Trump up close and personal during the campaign. Better than most, I knew where he was heading in national security. I knew his thinking on defense and foreign policy issues—and I thought he was correct. While many in the media made meaningless comments about his unworthiness to be the nation's commander in chief, I knew—from my experience in the military and business, and from my personal knowledge of him—that he was exactly the sort of leader we needed. I had no doubts about his capability. And I thought those who doubted him had failed to do their homework. If you read his books, from *The Art of the Deal* to *Time to Get Tough* to *Crippled America*, you would have a pretty good idea of his style, his way of approaching problems, and his commitment to success in business and for our country. Those who said that Donald J. Trump had no core beliefs were flat-out wrong. Anyone who read those books or who sat in meetings with him, where the discussions flew fierce and fast, would know that his nationalist-populist positions were thoroughly well grounded.

Stylistically, Trump is blunt. If someone walked into a room with an ugly dog, most of us would say, "That is an unusual animal, can you tell me about it?" Trump would more than likely say, "Wow, that is an ugly dog"—not with meanness but with candor. I appreciated his bluntness and personal honesty; I found him to be a very frank, open, and honest man. Many in Washington have a hard time dealing with people who don't deal in polite lies, establishment platitudes, and liberal talking points. Much of America found it refreshing, even if occasionally they would have preferred more diplomacy and tact.

Donald J. Trump trusts his instincts, because throughout his life they have served him well. He absorbs information rapidly and is quick in decision. He knows that it is better to decide than to delay; he trusts his gut to make the right decision with the information at hand—including the advice he has been given and questioned—rather than waiting for endless bureaucratic reports and waffling. In the military, I would constantly remind senior officers with years of experience to utilize their experience by trusting their instincts. The most successful leaders I knew did that. Military leaders build experience by sometimes having to make life-or-death decisions. That sharpens the mind and sense of responsibility. Trump gained enormous experience from constantly rubbing shoulders with blue-collar workers, inspecting buildings, interacting with staff, making it a point to talk with the masons, carpenters, cleaning staff, waiters, and bartenders who worked for him and the customers they served. He understood their lives, their needs, how they saw the world. He was anything but an elitist; he was, like Andrew Jackson, whose portrait prominently hung in the Oval, a populist leader who represented the interests of working- and middle-class Americans.

In Washington, which is full of lawyers and lobbyists, ideologues and propagandists and bureaucrats, this made him dangerous: dangerous because he didn't share the liberal consensus view; dangerous because he threw away current norms that weren't working—at least not working for the American people; dangerous because he was fearless in speaking out for what he saw as the truth. There is a metaphor in politics about touching the electrified "third rail," an issue that is so controversial that to discuss it is to risk one's political career. Donald Trump is the exceedingly rare politician willing to grab any and every third-rail issue if he thinks it needs to be dealt with.

As part of his diplomatic "art of the deal," Trump would call heads of state just to ask how they were doing. I was in the room when he called Russia's president, Vladimir Putin, to ask if he needed help with a massive fire in Siberia, a fire the size of Belgium. He would call South Africa's president, Cyril Ramaphosa, to see if his country needed ventilators during the early part of the COVID-19 pandemic. He would call Japan's prime minister, Shinzo Abe, when he became ill just to check in on him. Trump believes in the power of personal communications. He could be tough when defending American interests on calls with foreign leaders, but he also showed real friendship with the leaders of America's allies, and he took obvious enjoyment in learning about the issues with which other leaders were dealing. Of the many media misconceptions about the president, one of the greatest was certainly about his intellectual curiosity. His desire to learn was immense; he took pleasure in it.

In meetings, he asked many questions, and he probed every answer he was given. He always challenged the room. He forced people to refine their recommendations by seeing how they stood up against alternative premises. If you were not comfortable with this sort of Socratic conversation, you were in the wrong room. He was demanding and decisive—but he did not micromanage those charged with executing his plans.

We use the term "axis of advance" in the army. It describes a military maneuver, and a mindset, that is a general description of what the leader wants from his commanders, who are free to employ their own discretion and initiative in an attack. We also use the term "direction of attack," which is a specific direction a unit will use to attack and from which it will not deviate.

Trump's decisions and orders were more in line with an axis of advance. He gave cabinet officials plenty of latitude to solve problems, but he made very clear his desired end. These were often the issues on which he had written and campaigned. Too often, his subordinates thought their job was to change his mind or change the outcome.

The next foreign policy issue we faced was met by the president's team with surprising unity—and that was largely because of his leadership.

■ ■ ■

By 2017, Syria had been in a state of civil war for years. No matter how many times people assumed that Syria's dictator, Bashar al-Assad, was doomed to fall, he never did. He had most of the guns, he had Russian support, and he was determined to stay in power no matter what the cost.

United States policy under President Obama had been to provide covert aid to Syria's rebels while pushing for a diplomatic solution through the United Nations. A UN Security Council resolution (UNSCR 2254) called for a political solution to the conflict while providing hundreds of millions of dollars in humanitarian support.

Providing more than a billion dollars' worth of arms and logistical support was one thing, but President Obama had little stomach for committing American troops to another fight in the Middle East and tried to keep some distance from the conflict. In August 2012 reporters asked him under what circumstances he would commit to using direct American military force in Syria. Obama said, "We have been very clear to the Assad regime. A red line for us is we start seeing a whole bunch of chemical weapons moving around or being utilized."

Obama's self-proclaimed "red line" was crossed in August 2013, when the Assad regime used sarin nerve gas to kill more than a thousand men, women, and children in the suburbs of Damascus. There was no hiding what he had done, and Assad did not deny it. It was deliberate, brazen, and provocative. It was done in the face of what Assad clearly understood to be American policy; he just as clearly—and correctly—assumed that the Obama administration would do nothing. The actual response, as he apparently calculated, would only be moral outrage in the media and diplomatic protests by the American government. In the meantime, the regime, with the help of the Russians, maintained its stockpile of nerve gas—and Assad would use it again.

When it comes to weapons of war, none are "pretty." But nerve gas is horrific. Developed by the Nazis in World War II, but never used by them, sarin nerve gas is considered a weapon of mass destruction and is outlawed by the 1993 Chemical Weapons Convention. The Russians signed the 1993 convention; so did we. Syria acceded to the convention in 2013, apparently thinking the international community would, as so often, accept form over substance.

Early on the morning of 4 April 2017, I received a call summoning me to the White House Situation Room. Early morning calls never brought good news. This morning was no exception. Walking into the Situation Room from my West Wing office, I asked the senior duty officer what was happening. He told me that the intelligence agencies had assessed, with high confidence, that the Syrian military had conducted a chemical attack on a small town in northwest Syria called Khan Shaykhun. Initial reporting indicated that the Syrian military had used nerve gas against a civilian target; reported casualties were in the hundreds. The attack had been conducted during daylight hours with Russian-supplied jet fighter-bombers.

I went to the upper suite to inform the national security adviser, but McMaster was off-site at a speaking engagement. I took the short walk down to the Oval and told the president.

Going in, I knew he would not just say, "Thank you very much for informing me," but would ask me what I thought we should do. That was how he operated. He was action oriented; he would want my immediate opinion so he could start mulling it over and use it to solicit other opinions.

Sure enough, the president said, "What do you think?"

I said, "Mr. President, if the reports are true that the Syrians used nerve gas, it breaks all international norms. The Syrians did it during the Obama administration and the United States did nothing. If you do nothing, it will reinforce their belief that they can use weapons of mass destruction with no response from us. And it's not just Syria; the world is watching as well. We need to respond."

President Trump told me to call the secretary of defense. He wanted a full range of military and diplomatic options on his desk by that afternoon. Clear and to the point: classic Trump.

In Pentagon time, this timeline was beyond fast; it was almost unheard of. Usually the military cross-checks intelligence, gets recommended courses of action from the relevant combatant command, the senior military leadership meets to discuss the proposed actions, talking points are drawn up, the National Security Council is briefed and presented with options, and then approved recommendations reach the president. It can take days. This time, it all happened in hours. It was, as we were to call it, Trump time.

After calling Mattis and giving him a heads-up and leaving a message for McMaster via his traveling executive officer, I went over to the East Room to listen to the president give some remarks for a short ceremony. When the ceremony was completed, I ended up walking down the colonnade with the president and the vice president. The president had me reiterate my argument for taking military action against the Syrians not once but twice. It was one of his forms of cross-examination. If your second or third explanation differed from your first, he'd home in on that and ask why.

Standing between the president and vice president, I repeated, "A response by the United States will send a clear signal to the world that we will not tolerate the use of weapons of mass destruction—especially against defenseless civilian men, women, and children. The U.S. was challenged earlier, under Obama, when the Syrians used nerve gas—and we were found wanting. Our intelligence says that they have used sarin gas, which is illegal under international law. But no one will enforce that law except us. If we respond, forcibly, it will send a signal, early in your administration, that you are not afraid to drop gloves and fight, as they say in hockey. It will be a clear signal to the Russians too. They, through the Syrians, are testing you as well. And then there is Kim Jong Un in North Korea. He's also watching for your response. What signal will you send him?"

Hours later, in the White House Situation Room, Mattis briefed the commander in chief and the vice president on response options. I was there with McMaster and the chairman of the Joint Chiefs of Staff,

General Dunford. Also attending were Secretary of State Rex Tillerson, CIA director Mike Pompeo, Jared Kushner, Steve Bannon, and a few others. There was a robust discussion of a wide variety of options, ranging from a purely diplomatic protest to an aggressive missile attack.

Trump, in his usual style, asked questions that forced us to discuss the options among ourselves, making our own recommendations and critiquing others, while he challenged and judged the responses. If you were in the room, you would be asked not only for your opinion but for your response to other opinions. McMaster did not much care for open dialogue like this. He had called it a "scrum" when he first observed it in the Oval. He thought it was a disorderly way to do business, but it was classic Trump. No one could hide behind the fence post. And McMaster could not simply lecture as if he were a professor, which he was prone to do.

Trump pressed for an aggressive response. Mattis was cautious. It often appeared to me, in the months following the Yemen raid, that Mattis felt the need to be much more—indeed intensely—cautious in any recommendations for military action. Granted, this action, if carried out, could have much greater consequences. Russians were on the ground in Syria. They could be in the line of fire. Any action we took could dramatically heighten tension between Russia and the United States. Dunford and Tillerson fell more in line with Mattis in that we needed to be cautious. They each favored some sort of response; the question between them was what constituted an appropriate proportional response that would make our point without undue risk. Pompeo was bullish and all in for a significant missile strike. Kushner, sitting next to me, asked my opinion. I said, "If you use nerve gas on civilians you have crossed the line. If it were me, I would make the world notice. Even the Nazis never used sarin gas. We can't let it become acceptable now." Bannon argued against military action. He saw no point in America getting more deeply involved in the Syrian morass. Vice President Pence supported a moderate missile strike.

The president agreed with the vice president and opted for a missile strike at the Syrian airfield that had launched the attack. Our strike would be conservative, but with this warning to the Syrians: if there needed to be a next strike, that strike would be a lot stronger. Seven hours elapsed between President Trump's discovery of the Syrian gas attack to his response decision. And his decision was largely in line with the recommendation offered by Mattis and Dunford, in that the strike would be carefully targeted and arguably proportional to the provocation.

That afternoon the president flew to Mar-a-Lago. McMaster stayed with him. Deputy national security adviser K.T. McFarland and I remained with the vice president at the White House while Mattis and Dunford prepared the strike.

Orders went out, along with notifications to members of Congress and to our allies, and then we waited.

We assembled with Vice President Pence in the Situation Room in late evening. The president was in the secure room at Mar-a-Lago with Kushner, Tillerson, McMaster, Priebus, Mnuchin, and Bannon. Dunford was in the Pentagon and Mattis was on board the specialized E-4 aircraft known as the National Emergency Airborne Command Post. The story had not broken in the news. The operational security was solid. In the early morning of 7 April 2017, more than fifty Tomahawk land attack missiles, each with a thousand-pound blast warhead, slammed into Syria's Shayrat Air Base. Within minutes 20 percent of Syria's air force was out of action and the airfield badly damaged. The administration sent a clear message that, unlike the previous administration, we wouldn't stand by if Syria—or other countries—so egregiously violated international law as to use nerve gas against civilians. Trump was prepared to take further aggressive, dramatic action if necessary.

The international response was predictable. We had strong support from Israel and the United Kingdom. We had support with reservations from Germany and France. Our action was condemned by Russia and Iran.

The president had been decisive—and he had been right. If further proof were needed that America First did not mean isolationism, this was it. President Trump had showed decisive world leadership, as he would continue to do despite being dogged, for the entirety of his presidency, by a hostile press and a Democratic Party that wanted him impeached for perhaps the most absurd charges ever filed against a president.

CHAPTER TEN

Russia, Russia, Russia

I t was ironic, in a way, that this military action taken by the president was against Syria, a Russian ally, because if you listened to the media, President Trump was somehow a Russian stooge. The charge was utterly ridiculous and without foundation, but the media—and much of the Washington establishment—seemed to have lost its mind when Donald J. Trump won the presidency. The outcome was, to them, so improbable—not to say impossible—and horrible that there had to be some other—no matter how crazy—explanation. For Hillary Clinton, the media, and what became known as the "deep state" (the professional bureaucratic guardians of the liberal status quo), the answer was obviously that the Russians had somehow successfully conspired to put Donald J. Trump in the White House. Rumors, innuendo, and conspiracy theories were used by the media, the Democrats, and even parts of the United States government to harass the Trump administration through four years and two utterly uncalled-for impeachment hearings that were simply egregious political attacks on the president.

When Attorney General Jeff Sessions recused himself from a Justice Department investigation into Russian interference in the election campaign, he gave the deep state all the authority it needed to conduct this years-long harassment. Sessions allowed his deputy, Rod Rosenstein, to appoint former FBI director Robert Mueller to investigate "the Russian government's efforts to interfere in the 2016 presidential election." The investigation was, inevitably, a major distraction and a constant impediment to moving our agenda forward. Anyone who wasn't willingly self-deluded knew that any alleged collusion between the Trump campaign and the Russians was utterly bogus.

Ty Cobb, a flamboyant lawyer with a handlebar moustache, was brought into the White House to help handle issues related to the Mueller investigation. His office was next to mine in the West Wing.

Wandering into my office in late May, Ty asked, "Do you have a minute?" I told him sure and to sit down. After some polite talk he asked if I knew George Papadopoulos. I said yes and explained his role in the campaign. It seemed that the Mueller team thought Papadopoulos was some sort of key individual. I just laughed and told him everything he was reading about the investigation was garbage. If they were talking about collusion with the Russians, as small as our team was, it was a joke. "Heck," I said, "we had trouble colluding amongst ourselves." And Papadopoulos was more of a well-wisher than a key member of the campaign; he was a marginal figure on the distant periphery whose influence was effectively nil.

I got the feeling that Ty had something else on his mind, so I asked him, "What's up?"

"The Mueller team asked about your availability. We wanted you to be their first interview from the White House. Is that okay?"

"Yes." Actually, I couldn't wait.

"Do you have a lawyer? You might want to bring one."

"No, and I don't intend to hire one," I said. He looked at me like he was questioning my sanity, so I went on. "I know we did nothing wrong. I will tell the truth, and I don't need to hire someone to do that for me. If they don't like my answers, screw them." I remembered what my dad had told me years before: "Tell the truth and you only have to remember one story." I always thought that was good advice, and I never did hire a lawyer to help me with Mueller's investigators.

Ty asked me to call James Quarles on the Mueller team to set up a time for the interview. Quarles was a Mueller deputy and had been a well-known assistant special prosecutor for the Watergate Special Prosecution Force during the Nixon presidency. I called him and set up a meeting and told him I was coming alone, with no lawyer. Like Cobb, Quarles seemed surprised but said, "Okay."

Two days later I showed up at a nondescript federal building in Washington, D.C., that housed the Mueller team. Quarles met me in the lobby and walked me up to the fourth floor. I walked into a large room with a long interview table in the middle, where I was introduced to a team of seven investigators. They showed me their identification documents. Once we had been introduced and had sat down, I was told, "You are not a target of the investigation."

I was, as Cobb had intended me to be, the first interviewee from the White House and the national security team. I assumed my testimony would be the baseline from which the investigators would quiz K.T. McFarland, Hope Hicks, and the others. I didn't worry too much about that, because I was confident in what I knew, and I had no intention of going beyond what I knew. I knew enough to be certain that this investigation was an egregious waste of time and money, and was, whatever the intention of the investigators, pure political harassment of the president.

An FBI agent, the lead questioner, sat directly across from me. Another agent sat to my right. The other investigators took notes. I was interviewed for more than four hours about my work on the presidential campaign and with the presidential transition team.

As Cobb had suggested he would, the chief interrogator quickly focused the discussion on Papadopoulos. I told them how, at our one early official meeting of the ad hoc team of foreign policy advisers, Papadopoulos had introduced himself by saying he could arrange a meeting with Putin. Sessions had been immediately dismissive of his comment, Trump had shrugged it off, and I surmised that Papadopoulos was trying to puff himself up to appear far more connected and important than he was. In short, he was full of it.

After a bit more discussion, the FBI agent said, "He sounds like all hat and no cattle."

I replied, "That is a fair observation."

They asked if I knew about any type of Russian interaction with the campaign. I said no and told them that not once in any meeting or discussion I had with anyone at the campaign was there any mention of Russian collusion, Russian cooperation, or anything else about Russian involvement in the election.

The interview moved to the presidential transition and focused on Flynn's discussions with the Russian ambassador to the United States, Sergey Kislyak.

"Did you meet with him?"

I said no, not personally, but if I had, so what?

The FBI agent looked at me quizzically.

I said, "We were an authorized government transition office. We were the incoming administration. We had every right to be talking to ambassadors, political figures, reporters, you name it." There was nothing wrong with that; that's how transitions are done.

The FBI agent asked about other meetings we'd had, but his focus was clearly on Russia. He asked about discussions Ambassador Kislyak had had with Mike Flynn and K.T. McFarland about a United Nations vote in December 2016. Egypt had sponsored a United Nations Security Council vote on a resolution declaring, essentially, that Israeli settlements in the West Bank ("Palestinian territories occupied since 1967, including East Jerusalem") were in violation of international law. The Obama administration had a bad relationship with Israeli prime minister Benjamin Netanyahu, and it was well known that Netanyahu had welcomed Donald Trump's victory. Any permanent member of the Security Council could have defeated the resolution with a veto. Israeli officials had contacted Mike and K.T. because they were worried the Obama administration would not support Israel in the vote and asked if the incoming administration could do anything. Mike was candid. There is only one American president at a time. Though president-elect Trump was much more supportive of Israel, it was still President Obama's call about how the United States would vote in the Security Council. Mike and K.T. also talked with Russian ambassador Kislyak. The UN Security Council vote occurred on 23 December 2016. The United States abstained. Russia and every other member of the council voted for the resolution. If the Russians had wanted to gain favor with the incoming Trump administration, they could have voted against the resolution or, like the United States, abstained. But they did neither. How this was relevant to anything worthy of an FBI investigation was a mystery to me.

In the end, I think they merely wanted me to be defensive about our team's discussions with the Russians. But I was having none of it. I pushed back hard. We were the transition team of a newly elected president of the United States. We had government-issued phones, government laptop computers, and official government office space. We did not in any way interfere with the Obama administration, but we did what all transition teams do, which is prepare for as seamless as possible a transference of power, which included perfectly legal conversations with foreign ambassadors.

After my more than four-hour interview, I returned to the White House, briefed Ty, and told him I thought there had been no issues. I guess that was right because I was never called back. There had been no "aha!" moments.

Two weeks later, flying with the president on Air Force One, I went up to the forward compartment to go over a couple of issues with him. When we were done and I was walking out, the president stopped me and said, "I understand you spoke with the Mueller team."

I acknowledged I had and told him plainly that I thought it was a bogus investigation.

"Is it true you went into the meeting without a lawyer?"

"Yes."

He smiled and said, "I only know one or two others that would have the balls to do that."

He asked me nothing about the interrogators' questions, because I think, like me, he knew we had done nothing wrong. All we needed to do was tell the truth. (That was the mistake Mike Flynn had made—he let them intimidate him into lying.) To me, and to the president, the questions were in many ways irrelevant. He knew, as I did, that this was pure political harassment, and the best strategy was full cooperation, which the White House provided to the investigators.

In the end, the Mueller team employed nineteen lawyers and forty-five FBI agents to interview more than five hundred people. They issued 2,800 subpoenas and almost 500 search warrants. The White House provided 1.4 million documents and never once exerted executive privilege. The investigation took 675 days and cost $25 million. It was a truly colossal waste of time and money. Worse, it enflamed the media's hysteria and conspiracy mongering; it fed the worst instincts of the president's opponents; it did incalculable damage to the public's trust; and it impeded good governance by its very nature. It was a distraction that did not go unnoticed by foreign governments. The Mueller Report conceded that, "The investigation did not establish that members of the Trump Campaign conspired or coordinated with the Russian government in its election interference activities."

I could have saved them a lot of time and money. I knew that. I told them that. They didn't listen. They didn't care. What had actually happened during the campaign was not the point; the point was to pester President Trump's administration and make his job much more difficult.

CHAPTER ELEVEN

Endless War

When it came to national security, the longest-standing, most divisive issue was over our military policy in Afghanistan. Trump couldn't have been clearer that he wanted our troops home as soon as possible. We had "won" the war early on, and our continued involvement in supporting the Afghan government in its war against the Taliban was not, he believed, in the national interest. The money spent in Afghanistan was money that could be much better used at home. The American troops deployed in Afghanistan were risking their lives for negligible results. But the foreign policy establishment and its bureaucrats did everything to impede the president's goal of getting us out of Afghanistan. The president saw Afghanistan the way historians have long written about it—as the graveyard of empires—and he saw no reason to continue our involvement there. But for much of the foreign policy establishment, withdrawing from Afghanistan was virtually unthinkable, and that establishment very much included National Security Adviser H.R. McMaster and Secretary of Defense Jim Mattis. It was this issue, more than any other, that led the president to distrust their advice and doubt their candor.

Everyone knew where Trump stood. He was not ambiguous about it. He spoke about it often, both publicly and privately. During the campaign, Trump asked me repeatedly why we were still in Afghanistan. He saw no point to it. I told him that we had eliminated the direct terrorist threat to us—al Qaeda—years ago, and we were no longer there to win a war, but to build a nation in the midst of a civil war. The foreign policy establishment used that civil war—and the possibility of the anti-government, Islamist forces of the Taliban winning it—as a rationale for staying in Afghanistan, perhaps in perpetuity. Trump inevitably followed up with more questions, which always led him back to a question that was more of a statement: "Then why are we still there? It makes no sense; this is not in our vital national interest; we're wasting money and our soldiers' lives."

My ultimate conclusion, which I told him, was that we were there for two reasons: "habit and generals." Foreign policy analysts are as driven by habit as anyone else, and no general wanted to be held responsible for "losing" Afghanistan. Our continuing involvement in Afghanistan made little military or geostrategic sense, but a generation of officers grew up fighting and serving in Afghanistan, and being there became a habit. My youngest son, Tyler, was in middle school when we invaded Afghanistan in 2001. He served there as a young officer with the 82nd Airborne Division. My daughter served in Afghanistan. My son-in-law served in Afghanistan. When the Soviets invaded Afghanistan in 1979, I was involved in helping to arm their Afghan opponents as part of our Cold War foreign policy against communism. Back then we all recognized that Afghanistan was one of the worst places to have to fight a war. We did not envy the Soviets; in fact, we took grim satisfaction that they were trapped in a war in a landlocked country roughly the size of Texas, with rugged terrain, surrounded by six countries that could provide sanctuary for their opponents. The Afghans were raised in a warrior culture, and their country was not "target rich." As one wag said, you would have to bomb Afghanistan *up* to the Stone Age. And yet, here we were now, in Afghanistan ourselves, trying to turn it into a Muslim liberal democracy. The president was right to be skeptical about the wisdom of our continued involvement there.

Trump believed, rightly, that Afghanistan was a distraction to any coherent America First global strategy. He saw that we needed to pivot from the relatively small, containable threat of Afghan-based Islamist terrorism to the far greater threat of China, which was our real foreign policy rival in the world (and a much more serious economic-military threat than Russia, by the way).

On several occasions during the campaign, Trump asked me for a strategy on how to end America's longest war. I told him that the key was to give his national security adviser, secretary of defense, secretary of state, and chairman of the Joint Staffs a deadline by which all American troops would be withdrawn. He needed to hold them to this deadline and not let them hide behind an alleged need for arranging the right "conditions" before we left, because the conditions would never be right, they would keep changing, and the goal would never be met. My words were prophetic. We got bogged down with an endless set of changing conditions laid down by the president's national security advisers.

McMaster had served in Afghanistan. His view of the conflict differed sharply from the president's. His priority was not withdrawing American troops; it was backing the Afghan government, which was in a long-standing civil war that it was losing. In his own words, McMaster thought the prospect of American troops leaving Afghanistan to be "abhorrent."

Trump wanted things done quickly, and that included getting American troops out of Afghanistan. McMaster moved slowly, hoping that events would work themselves out. He and Secretary of Defense Mattis and Secretary of State Tillerson would nod their heads as if in agreement with the president about the need to bring our troops home, but in truth they wanted no part of any exit from Afghanistan. They believed that American withdrawal meant the Taliban would take over the country. Such an outcome, they thought, would pose a grave threat to our national security. But the real question was which threat was greater: spending our blood and treasure endlessly in Afghanistan, or letting the Afghan civil war reach a conclusion—and dealing with that conclusion as we needed to?

President Trump and Vice President Pence believed that the situation in Afghanistan was a strategic stalemate (which it was), that current policy set no standards for when American troops could ever leave, and that having run on the issue of removing American troops from conflicts that served no national interest, they intended to see American troops withdrawn from Afghanistan at the earliest responsible date.

But nearly all the leading members of the administration's national security team opposed administration policy. Instead, Mattis, McMaster, Tillerson, and the Joint Chiefs invoked what I called the three Ts strategy: "More Troops; More Time; Trust Us." The president always asked, "How much more time? How many more troops? How will additional time and troop deployments alter the outcome? Is there a strategy for victory?" His trust visibly waned as it appeared that their desired timeline seemed to stretch to infinity.

Still, in the first year of his administration, Trump resolved that he would give his generals a chance. He had, after all, appointed Mattis secretary of defense, he had selected McMaster to be his national security adviser, he had renominated General Dunford as chairman of the Joint Chiefs of Staff, and he had made General John Kelly his chief of staff after having first chosen him to head the Department of Homeland Security. They all pushed the three Ts strategy. The president doubted it would work, but he reluctantly agreed to a temporary increase in troop strength. He made it clear that he was not doing so in the interests of "nation-building." He acceded to his generals' advice in the hope that it would establish better conditions for an eventual American withdrawal.

Unknowingly, the generals had set a trap for themselves. They put forward a plan that was in fact merely a continuation of the status quo. It could not, as the president surmised, deliver the positive results they claimed. They effectively undid the president's trust in their judgment.

Later on in the administration, I invited foreign policy analyst and writer Robert Kaplan to talk with the vice president. There were many issues on which Kaplan and I differed, but the Trump White House was always willing to listen to alternative points of view, and there were some fundamental foreign policy questions about which Kaplan and I absolutely agreed. One was his statement to the vice president: "U.S. militaries do not do well in fixing complex Islamic societies." I remembered my work with the Coalition Provisional Authority in Baghdad and thought, "Yep, been there, done that." I had my own conclusions, which I told anyone who would listen: "We are not Afghans. It is their country. If we don't have a solution in hand to their political problems, after having had troops in their country since 2001, maybe our approach is wrong; maybe it's time for us to get out and let them resolve the issues themselves."

It wasn't until Mike Pompeo became secretary of state in April 2018 that the president had someone with cabinet-level authority who was dedicated to promoting his agenda and who had the ability both to challenge the Pentagon and the national security adviser and to take authority away from them. John Bolton became national security adviser the same month that Pompeo took office. Bolton, like his predecessors, believed in maintaining an American presence in Afghanistan, but Pompeo, like Trump, thought we had room for a diplomatic maneuver. The president said he wanted a negotiator to end the war in Afghanistan. Thanks to Pompeo, he finally got one.

In September 2018, Pompeo appointed Zalmay Khalilzad, a veteran American diplomat and an old Afghan hand, to be the U.S. special representative for Afghan reconciliation. He would be our lead for peace discussions with the Taliban. Zal, who was born and raised in Afghanistan, is an ethnic Pashtun, as are the Taliban, and he and Pompeo saw a diplomatic path for ending America's longest war. Zal would act as an intermediary between the Afghan government and the Taliban and report directly to Pompeo.

In late 2018, Pompeo negotiated the release of Taliban leader Abdul Baradar from the Pakistani jail where he had been held since 2010.

Before his imprisonment, Baradar had been the second-ranking leader in the Taliban after Mullah Omar, and he had been publicly announced as Omar's heir apparent. Zal knew Baradar. He knew that Baradar had been open to a negotiated settlement. It was a bold diplomatic move to get him released so that we could negotiate an end to the war. We took it, and in less than a year, Zal Khalilzad and Abdul Baradar had achieved a rough outline for a negotiated peace between the United States and the Taliban.

In August 2019, Zal briefed the president on the plan, which would mean that all U.S. troops would be withdrawn from Afghanistan by October 2020. At last, President Trump had his goal in sight, but he still asked questions. He asked Gina Haspel, his director of the Central Intelligence Agency, about the potential danger of al Qaeda regenerating itself in Afghanistan. If al Qaeda attempted that, how long would it take? Haspel said three years, if the Taliban let them. The president probed for every potential weakness in the agreement. It was not perfect, no peace agreement ever is, but Zal made a convincing case that it was in our interest and could be made to work.

John Bolton attended this meeting, which was held at Trump's Bedminster, New Jersey, golf course, and flew back with us on Air Force Two. I commented to Vice President Pence that Zal had done good work and that this agreement on Afghanistan could have been had two years ago if Tillerson, Mattis, and McMaster had supported the president's policy directives. Bolton said nothing. Shortly thereafter, he told the president, the vice president, and the secretary of state that he totally disagreed with Zal's work. It caught everyone by surprise given his previous silence. Trump had already begun to sour on Bolton based on missteps on policy discussions involving North Korea, Iran, and Venezuela. He was not on the same page as the president. President Trump fired Bolton on 10 September 2019.

Institutional resistance slowed the negotiations, but by 29 February 2020 the United States had an official agreement to end the Afghan War, with the last American troops scheduled to be out on 1 May 2021. The president asked me to keep an eye on developments in Afghanistan and to let him know if there was an opportunity to move more quickly. If there was, he wanted to take it. As it was, I provided the president with weekly updates on our troop withdrawals and weekly confirmations that the Taliban was honoring the peace agreement by not attacking our troops. No American troops were killed by the Taliban after the February agreement and through the rest of our administration. Trump had reinforced our concern by personally speaking with Mullah Baradar on two occasions from the Oval Office.

At the time, our intelligence reports indicated that the Taliban was in its strongest position since 2001. The Afghan government had done little if any contingency planning for how it would defend itself after United States troops, and the troops of our NATO allies, departed. The policy of Afghanistan's president, Ashraf Ghani, seemed based entirely on the hope that we would not leave, and that we would forever fight the government's battles for them. In a poll conducted by the U.S. Department of State, 73 percent of Afghans wanted peace. It was well past time for a negotiated settlement. We knew it, and President Ghani needed to accept it.

When President Trump was inaugurated, there were 10,355 U.S. troops in Afghanistan. Under the recommendations of Mattis, Tillerson, and McMaster that number grew to 16,414. When the president received intelligence assessments that these troop additions had not changed the character of the war, he pushed hard for peace negotiations with the Taliban, resulting in the agreement of 29 February 2020. By November 2020 we were at 4,512 troops. The withdrawal was orderly and successful, and when the president asked me if we could accelerate it, I said we could, but advised against it, because I couldn't speak for the consequences. The pace at which we were moving was guided by intelligence and military assessments.

On 17 November 2020, President Trump signed his final presidential decision memorandum on Afghanistan. He had wanted to have all American troops home by Inauguration Day, but, guided by our advice, he set a goal of reducing the troop level to 2,500 by 20 January 2021 and all out by 1 May. By 8 January 2021, we had reached the lowest number of troops in Afghanistan since the start of the war nineteen years earlier, and the Taliban had not killed a single American since the signing of our peace agreement. Of the many unheralded accomplishments of the Trump administration, this one was, for our troops, surely one of the most important. The plan to end our longest war was working and on track. All the new administration had to do was execute the coordinated plan we left them.

CHAPTER TWELVE

Defeating ISIS and Dealing with "Little Rocket Man"

I n the military, we sometimes talk about near targets (that you need to engage early) and far targets (that can wait). The president and I regarded ISIS as a near target.

The Islamic State of Iraq and Syria (ISIS) had been around for a long time. It was founded in 1999 by a Jordanian terrorist, Abu Musab al-Zarqawi. It gained adherents in the aftermath of the Iraq War, but outside the world of counter-terrorism experts it remained a little-known extremist group. In 2014 President Obama referred to ISIS as a terrorist JV (junior varsity) team. Two years later, though, ISIS had grown to be the world's most brutal terrorist network, controlling an area larger than Great Britain and holding major cities like Mosul in Iraq and Raqqa in Syria.

I saw ISIS as a dangerous exporter of terrorism that needed to be crushed right away. On 28 January 2017, eight days after he was sworn in, President Trump signed a national security presidential memorandum directing his national security team to develop a plan within thirty days to defeat the Islamic State of Iraq and Syria. It contained a simple statement: "It is the policy of the United States that ISIS be defeated."

The Defense and State Departments hit their deadlines for developing a plan to defeat ISIS. During a briefing on 27 February 2017, Mattis told the president that we had two options. One involved the deployment of ten thousand U.S. troops. The other relied on surrogate militias, especially the Syrian Democratic Forces (SDF). I knew from my previous conversations with the president that he favored a solution that relied heavily on local forces. Mattis got the green light to work with the SDF to destroy ISIS. That was the general strategy, and the president put no restrictions on how Mattis was to go about achieving it. Defeating ISIS meant rendering it unable "to achieve operational effects through coordinated actions from safe havens" and rendering it "unable to control critical populations and key terrain." That might sound like nonsensical jargon, but it was actually a militarily achievable objective that I defined as "defeat"—and that, and the president's support of the effort, made all the difference.

We would work through dual paths. The United States Army would support Iraqi forces as they reduced Mosul, while we would use United States, French, and British Special Operations forces to support the Syrian Democratic Forces in Syria in reducing ISIS. And we would provide massive air support.

The SDF was half Arab and half Kurd, led by a Kurdish general known by his nom de guerre, Mazloum. Turkey's president, Recep Tayyip Erdogan, considered Mazloum and the SDF as terrorists. It was President Trump's job to convince him otherwise. To Erdogan, if you were Kurdish and had a weapon, you were PKK, which was a Kurdish militant organization in Turkey. Erdogan complained about our support for the SDF, but in the end Trump listened to Erdogan's objections, rejected them, and remained, at the end of his four years in office, one of the very few NATO country leaders who had a good relationship with Erdogan. This is because he recognized that Turkey, a NATO ally, has its own national interests in the area—interests that will be longer lasting than our own—because Turkey borders Syria. When President Trump was accused of later "abandoning" the Kurds, he did nothing of the sort.

He used Turkey, as opposed to American troops, as a buttress against expanding Russian influence in Syria. That's called strategy.

In the meantime, we executed the Trump-approved plan and began clawing back territory from ISIS. By the end of July 2017, American-supported Iraqi forces retook the city of Mosul in brutal urban combat. By October, Raqqa had fallen to our allies. ISIS was collapsing, its sadistic leader, Abu Bakr al-Baghdadi, was in hiding, and his "caliphate" had been destroyed. For the next two years we relentlessly tracked ISIS's leader until we found him.

In late October 2019, Secretary of Defense Mark Esper, chairman of the Joint Chiefs General Mark Milley, CIA director Gina Haspel, and National Security Adviser Robert O'Brien told the president and vice president in the residence's Yellow Oval that Baghdadi had been located. He was hiding with his extended family in a villa near Barisha, Syria. Our intelligence agencies had "high confidence" he was there. We needed a quick decision, because if operational security was broken—and any delay brought with it the risk of leaks—it might take another two years to find him. There were two options: dropping a guided bomb into the compound or launching a Special Operations ground attack. The ground assault was the only way we could confirm it was Baghdadi, but there was greater risk to American lives. The president looked at his newly confirmed chairman of the Joint Chiefs and said, "General, what do you think?" Milley's response: "Ground assault." The decision from the president was immediate: "Okay, let's go." It was to be a ground assault as soon as possible, using army special operators from Delta Force, supported by Task Force 160 and the U.S. Air Force.

On a cool Sunday in late October, a select group of presidential advisers filed into the White House Situation Room. An army Delta Squadron was moving into position to execute Operation Kayla. The mission's name was to honor a young American woman, Kayla Mueller, who had been brutalized and killed by Baghdadi years earlier.

Sitting in the Situation Room, we watched the operation unfold. Our troops broke into the compound, and a military dog chased

Baghdadi into an underground tunnel, where the terrorist blew himself up, along with two children. The assault force left nothing to chance. It extracted Baghdadi's body; forensics confirmed his identity; and, eventually, his remains, like bin Laden's, were buried at sea. After our troops were extracted, the compound was destroyed by an air strike so it could not become a shrine or gathering point. There were no American casualties. From the identification of Baghdadi's location to the execution of the strike took less than a week. It was, again, classic Trump decision making: fast and firm.

Kayla Mueller, for whom the operation was named, had been active overseas in humanitarian relief work. She was kidnapped by ISIS in 2013. As a Christian, she was made to suffer for her faith. Her mother said in a *Newsweek* interview that her daughter would still be alive if President Obama had been as decisive as President Trump had been. I got to know Kayla's parents during the 2020 reelection campaign. Her father, Carl Mueller, told me that he didn't think anything would have stopped President Trump from getting Baghdadi. I agreed. Trump was decisive—and he was determined to take out ISIS and its evil leader.

■ ■ ■

While President Trump and I agreed that ISIS was America's biggest threat in 2016 and 2017, most political pundits (and some officials within his own administration, like Secretary of State Rex Tillerson) would have had a different answer. They would have pointed to North Korea, its growing nuclear arsenal, and its push to develop intercontinental ballistic missiles capable of hitting the United States. North Korea's conventional military hardware is declining toward obsolescence, but it offsets this disadvantage through sheer manpower (it has, by some measurements—if one includes paramilitary units—the largest military in the world); terrorism (it is a state sponsor of terrorism); and other "asymmetric capabilities," most especially its nuclear program and its possible stockpile of chemical and biological weapons.

It seemed that every time North Korean dictator Kim Jong Un wanted our attention, he would launch a short- or medium-range missile. The missiles would strike into the Sea of Japan or into the greater Pacific Ocean; whenever that happened, I'd get a call from the White House Situation Room.

Near eleven o'clock Monday night, on 25 September 2017, my secure phone rang in my home office. Late night calls, like early morning ones, never brought good news. A week earlier, Kim Jong Un had fired another ballistic missile over Japan, landing two thousand miles farther east into the Pacific Ocean. But this time, the call I received was not from the Situation Room; it was from the president of the United States. He wanted to talk about North Korea and Kim Jong Un. He wanted to know my thoughts about what we should do with "Little Rocket Man."

I believed that "Little Rocket Man," as the president called him, was not a pressing threat. My preference was always to fight "one war at a time." Our priority, I thought, should be extracting ourselves from one war (Afghanistan) and winning another (against ISIS) largely using surrogates. (Little did I know that we would soon face another political "battle" with the Mueller investigation and continual threats of impeachment.)

I did not deny that North Korea posed a threat. It manifestly did, and has been a threat since its first nuclear test in 2006. Its growing nuclear capability is one very big reason why we have ground-based interceptor missiles in Alaska and California. But I believed that North Korea was a manageable threat—certainly manageable by President Trump, who is a tough and gifted negotiator, one who would jealously guard our own security while being unafraid to launch new diplomatic initiatives.

North Korea is called a "hermit kingdom"—and for very good reason. The North Korean regime isolates its people from the world. Its Communist economy punishes its people with poverty and slave labor. The state bombards the people with propaganda and monitors them relentlessly. Gathering intelligence from this police state is difficult.

Negotiating with the North Koreans is even more difficult. The North Korean manner of negotiating is based on lies, threats, obstructions, demands, and delays—and that's when they're being cooperative. No previous administration had been able to crack this hermit kingdom and extract concessions that would lower the threat level. For example, when Donald Trump was elected president, the Korean peninsula was still technically in a state of war (dating from the Korean War), with only an armistice between the warring factions. Many in the military thought that a war with North Korea was both imminent and inevitable. The North Korean regime was so aggressive and reckless that it would hit a trip wire, strike Japan or South Korea, and bring the United States into a major conventional war.

But the president and I took a more hopeful view. The president felt he had diplomatic cards to play, and 2017 was a quiet year of back-channel diplomacy. Trump began by continuing what previous administrations had done—attempting to apply pressure on North Korea through China. He maintained economic sanctions. He maintained our military presence in the area. He carried on most of the diplomatic initiatives previous administrations had pursued, but the president did not expect that these initiatives would achieve any diplomatic breakthroughs with North Korea—after all, they had not worked for previous administrations. But while he kept these traditional approaches open, he innovated another. He made the matter of North Korean diplomacy personal. Big, long-winded meetings with North Korean diplomats browbeating our diplomats were out, personal diplomacy was in. Trump met North Korea's fiery rhetoric with his own. He publicly mocked Kim Jong Un. He engaged in an undiplomatic diplomatic approach that the North Koreans did not expect. And he knew exactly what he was doing. He had read his man in Kim Jong Un. Trump showed he would not be bullied. He openly bragged that he held the bigger hand economically and militarily. When Kim Jong Un said that his nuclear launch button was "always on my table," Trump said, "My nuclear button is bigger and more powerful." Many in the press were apoplectic, but Trump knew exactly what he was doing. He also knew, through South Korean back channels, that Kim Jong Un wanted to meet him. That was the sort of breakthrough he was willing to exploit. Trump made it clear that he was willing to do something that no other president had ever done. He was willing to meet with the leader of North Korea.

Speaking with his entire national security team on 11 January 2018, he told them, "I want you to look at the world differently." He brought that style to his discussions with North Korea. In one Oval Office meeting, he asked whether we should try to do more on North Korea. I told him, no. On the contrary, I thought we were trying to do too much; our expectations were set too high. A total, fully verifiable nuclear stand-down by North Korea was not going to happen. For Kim Jong Un, being a nuclear power was the only thing that made him internationally important; he also likely viewed it as his one assurance that his regime could never be taken down. The idea—once broadcast in public by John Bolton—that the United States was considering the "Libya model" for North Korean denuclearization was not supported by Trump, who said, "The Libya model isn't a model we have at all" for North Korea. Bolton's comment almost caused the North Koreans to stop talking with us. Maybe that is what he actually wanted. The Libya model demanded disarmament first, compensation later, and finally, for Libya's then leader Muammar Gaddafi, ended in his overthrow and death. I told President Trump that Kim Jong Un would never accept that outcome as a good "model." Trump agreed. No "supreme ruler" could possibly think the Libyan model was a good one; he would view it as the vindication of his every fear.

In May 2018, President Trump sent his new secretary of state, Mike Pompeo, to Pyongyang for a meeting that lasted ten hours. Our diplomatic efforts were gaining definite traction, and other world leaders noticed. On 5 May 2018, British prime minister Theresa May told President Trump that he "had done better than any president before" in making diplomatic progress with the North Koreans. A few days later, even President Xi of China would say, "You have led us well" in the matter of North Korea, and that Kim Jong Un had "expectations" that a diplomatic agreement with the United States could be in the offing. Easier spoken than done, but, still, in the past, such optimism had been exceedingly rare when it came to North Korea.

As Pompeo noted, the diplomatic issues with North Korea were compounded because "they do not know how to do this"—that is, negotiate constructively. North Korea had never had such high-level discussions as were being proposed between North Korea and the United States. They simply did not know how to engage with a Western power and conduct a meeting that wasn't pure Communist agitational-propaganda theater. Pompeo thought Kim Jong Un was eager for a deal that would raise his status in the world from leader of a pariah nation to a leader respectable enough to meet with the president of the United States. It would be a complicated, contentious, and cumbersome process given the nature of the North Korean regime, but Trump wanted a summit meeting to happen and thought it was worth whatever diplomatic risks were entailed. In a cabinet meeting on 9 May 2018, he said that a summit meeting with Kim Jung Un would be "a victory for the world."

President Trump was very involved in the negotiations leading up to the summit. Trump wanted Kim Jong Un to understand two salient points. First, this was an opportunity for him to lead his nation into peace and prosperity. Second, the United States and North Korea could be the best of friends—with all that could mean in terms of trade and economic development—or the worst of enemies. It would be Kim Jong Un's call based on his willingness to cooperate with the United States. President Trump told me that he suspected the summit had "a 70 percent risk of failure" in the sense that we would likely walk away without a denuclearization agreement. "I'm prepared for that," the president said. But he also thought the potential gain in lowering tensions with North Korea, limiting its nuclear program, and achieving some sort of manageable détente with the regime was well worth any political risk he was running.

The president told everyone not to invoke the "Libyan model," but to instead compare our goals with North Korea to the "Kazakhstan model." The Kazakhstan regime had inherited nuclear weapons from the former Soviet Union. Kazakhstan agreed to denuclearize in return for the United States, the United Kingdom, and Russia signing a memorandum guaranteeing Kazakhstan's sovereignty and security.

Not for the first time, I thought the president had a better understanding of diplomacy and negotiation than did some of his leading foreign policy advisers. While Bolton had proposed a model that, presumably, ended in Kim Jong Un's overthrow and execution, Trump insisted on a model that offered him survival and security if he agreed to reduce or eliminate his stockpile of nuclear weapons.

As we approached early June, the summit was still in doubt. The North Koreans couldn't help but revert to form and be obstructive and uncooperative. We were advised by those who studied the North Korean regime that our chances of achieving a meeting were very small. The North Koreans could trumpet our willingness to have a meeting as a sign of their prestige. Their refusal to consent to meet with us could be propagandized as a sign of their superiority.

I told the president to trust his instincts, as they had brought us to this point. Sure enough, a week later, with China's blessing and with Prime Minister Lee Hsien Loong of Singapore acting as a superb host, Kim Jong Un and President Donald J. Trump had their summit meeting. The first-ever meeting between the two leaders could not have gone better. Coming back from the summit on Air Force One, the president made two immediate calls. The first was to President Moon Jae In of South Korea, who congratulated the president for setting the table for future talks, an outcome that "exceeded my expectations." The second phone call went to Japanese prime minister Shinzo Abe, who congratulated President Trump on "truly a historic meeting."

In February 2019, there was a second summit meeting between Kim Jong Un and President Trump. This time it was in Hanoi, Vietnam. President Trump was seriously committed to hammering out an agreement, but equally serious about walking away if he felt an agreement could not be reached that was in America's best interests. The North Koreans miscalculated. They thought that they could behave as they had done in the past and make extraordinary demands. Trump cut them short. In fact, at Trump's request, a scheduled lunch was canceled, and the summit ended early. Trump stated, "Sometimes you have to walk. This was just one of those times." He thought the North Koreans had shown a lack of seriousness in their negotiations. So, he called their bluff and called off the summit. That the North Koreans were surprised would, I think, be an understatement. But they respected Trump, back-channel negotiations continued, and in June 2019, President Trump made history again when he crossed over the Korean Demilitarized Zone, met Kim Jong Un on North Korean soil, and then presided over a brief meeting with him and South Korean president Moon Jae In, which resulted in a North Korean promise to renew negotiations for the denuclearization of the Korean peninsula.

Though it was rarely commented upon in the press, Trump's personal diplomacy resulted in a clear reduction in military tensions between North and South Korea. Relations between North Korea and the United States, while not exactly warm, were better than they had ever been—and all without America making any economic or military concessions. Indeed, the concessions came from North Korea, which muted its anti-American propaganda and made efforts, on its own, to continue talks with the United States. Had Trump been elected to a second term, I believe his progress in working for the denuclearization of North Korea would have achieved even more success.

CHAPTER THIRTEEN

National Security Adviser to the Vice President

On 26 April 2018, I did something I hardly ever did. It was a nice spring day, and I decided to step outside the White House complex and get a sandwich. I needed a brief break, a leave-me-alone moment. As soon as my sandwich arrived, so did a phone call.

I normally carried two phones (my "official" phone and my private phone), three if traveling (the third was a "secure" phone). Both my official and private phones rang with calls from the Situation Room. I took the call on my official phone. The watch officer said, "Sir, you are wanted in the Oval, now." I literally ran out of the restaurant, leaving the sandwich, untouched, on its plate.

I made my way through the Secret Service checkpoints, did a fast walk into the West Wing, and was pointed into the Oval Office. The president and his chief of staff, John Kelly, and the vice president and his chief of staff, Nick Ayers, were gathered around a table in the small presidential dining room, where Trump did most of his work, surrounded by stacks of papers and books, and with a television on above the small fireplace.

I wasn't out of breath, but I was close, and my brain was racing through everything going on in the world. Had they called me because of an issue in the Middle East, Afghanistan, Iraq, Syria, Europe, NATO, the Far East, China, North Korea, South America? National Security Adviser John Bolton was not in the room, so I was on my own.

The president said, "Keith, Mike has a question for you."

Everyone was grinning, which I found even more confusing.

Vice President Pence said, "I would like you to be my national security adviser."

I was dumbfounded and said nothing.

Finally, the vice president said, "Well, why don't you sleep on it and let's talk tomorrow."

"No, sir, I would love to do it. That's just the very last question I thought I would be asked."

Everyone laughed.

President Trump said, "Both of you shake on it."

We did.

Chief of Staff General Kelly said, "You will still be an assistant to the president." That was important, because it meant I was still classified as a member of the White House senior staff with access to the president. The vice president would now have two APs (assistants to the president): his chief of staff and me.

President Trump added, "I'll still want to pull you into meetings when I need your advice."

Still in a bit of a daze, I went down the hall to see John Bolton. I told him, "I think I just got fired and hired at the same time."

He laughed and said, "I knew this was coming." The president wanted the vice president's national security adviser to be someone he knew and trusted—and that was me.

On my first Monday on the job, the vice president gave me my marching orders: "Keep me informed and keep me ready." And, he added, "Unless the president has directed otherwise, you will be in all the meetings you would previously have attended with the president." I was, in some ways, the national security and foreign policy bridge between the two offices, and that put me in a great position to compare and contrast the president and the vice president and provide consistent recommendations to both.

I have always made a close study of leaders and managers. Throughout my years in the military and business worlds, I have been fortunate. I have worked for the best of the best when it comes to leadership. In the military, the leaders I worked with were almost uniformly superb. It was only after I left the military that I came to witness questionable and downright bad leadership and management. Some of that was in business. But there was a lot of it in politics, where disloyalty, cold-blooded ambition, ideological feuds, and countless other counterproductive behaviors were just a fact of life. But both President Trump and Vice President Pence were, in their very different ways, highly effective leaders and managers.

In the four years of the Trump-Pence administration I was the only senior official (as an assistant to the president) who played a key supporting role to both men. I came up with my own nicknames, not approved by the U.S. Secret Service, for the president and vice president. They called them "Mogul" and "Hoosier." I called them "Fire" and "Ice."

President Trump was an immensely consequential president. His election was a "black swan" event—winning against all odds on a platform that created a new, more populist Republican Party. The Trump-reformed Republican Party is an America First party, opposed to the liberal consensus and fully aware that liberalism is sliding dangerously to the far left.

As for Trump himself, he fires on all cylinders, all the time, and is utterly fearless. He says what he thinks, hits back at his critics, and fully embraces the idea of politics as a contact sport. Not only does Trump always speak his mind, but you had better be ready for his questions. He wanted his advisers to speak their minds too, plainly, openly, and with enough forethought that whatever we said would withstand sustained scrutiny. You could disagree with him—he welcomed that—but you had better be armed with a compelling point. To me, Trump's manner was exceptionally refreshing. It is what voters responded to during the campaign. They saw him as a man who didn't speak in platitudes or with insincerity. He didn't represent the bipartisan status quo that stood for liberal international trade (regardless of its costs to American jobs and manufacturing), foreign nation-building (regardless of its costs to American lives and treasure), and a leftward drift in domestic policy (regardless of its costs in undermining America's constitutional laws and ideals). He, and the people who supported him, recognized that America was on the wrong course. Because he was unbeholden to traditional politicians, he was uniquely positioned, as he would say himself, to fix what ailed the country. Trump voters wanted a fighter in the White House. They were fed up with go-along, get-along Republicans who wanted to be popular with the media, who wanted to be bipartisan, and so embraced at least half the liberal agenda. Trump set his own agenda—and he fought for it. He was a near unstoppable force of nature. He was "Fire."

I loved being around the president. I know many were put off by his style. But when people told me that they thought he was impolite or offensive or whatever their criticisms were, I asked them to take a look at the president's children. These were the people who knew him better than anyone else—the public man and the private man. And they adore him. Ask yourself, honestly, why?

You might also consider his wife, Melania. Gracious and spectacular in her carriage and beauty, she is the president's closest confidante. The Secret Service code name for her was "Muse." When she was in meetings, she was unafraid to make her position known, and her opinions were always grounded in common sense. She was a wonderful ambassador for the White House, did excellent charitable work, and saw through the hypocrisy of the media. She knows, as well as anyone, that her husband is a much better man than the media made him appear. Yes, Trump can be aggressive. Yes, he can be profane. Yes, he is willing to say publicly things that many of us would only say in private or keep to ourselves. On more than one occasion, I heard him say something that made people wince, even if they later acknowledged it was true. Yes, he could be a showman—more of a showman than some wanted in a president. But that showmanship was undeniably effective, as witness his campaign rallies. He is also extremely intelligent, if blunt; funny, though the media often missed the joke; candid, perhaps to a fault; and caring, in a way that few were willing to recognize except privately. His spats were public, his compassion largely private. His interest in and concern for other people, especially working people, went deep. His core driving principal is loyalty and I see nothing wrong with that. He demands it—and he returns it when he is well served. Loyalty is what wins battles and loyalty is needed when the nights are the darkest. Anyone who tells you otherwise does not understand leadership.

We sometimes forget that Winston Churchill was, in his day, distrusted by the political establishment, regarded as outrageously frank, belligerent in rhetoric, stubborn in defending unpopular positions he believed in, and unafraid of criticism. I know many will scoff at the comparison, but I do believe there are strong parallels between Trump and Churchill. Churchill said this about loyalty: "When we are debating an issue, loyalty means giving me your honest opinion, whether you think I will like it or not. But once a decision is made, debate ends. Loyalty then means executing the decision as if it were your own." Trump believed that. He was ill served by political appointees who did not.

One day in May 2018, the president and I had a wide-ranging discussion, one that went far beyond national security and foreign policy issues. In that conversation he conceded that he sometimes used "nasty rhetoric" but let me know that he did it deliberately to label opponents, put them on the defensive, and unnerve them. He recognized that "language always plays a part" in any politician's arsenal. Barack Obama once said, repurposing a line from the movie *The Untouchables*, "If they bring a knife to the fight, we bring a gun." No one was ever going to verbally outdraw Donald Trump.

Trump is endlessly energetic, always open to discussions, and unflaggingly optimistic. This reflexive openness and optimism are grounded in self-confidence. Self-confidence and optimism are important leadership qualities that I looked for in young officers. When the fat is in the fire, lives are at risk, and enemy fire is raining down, you want leaders who are confident, positive, and looking to make the best of their circumstances. As I once told my paratroopers in the 82nd Airborne, getting dropped behind enemy lines is great; it means we get to fight in any direction we want. There is something to be said for confidence.

I am still surprised, though I shouldn't be, at how viciously the media criticized Trump for his optimism during the Wuhan coronavirus pandemic. It was part of their narrative that the president was uninformed, propagating false hope, and pursuing quack remedies. In fact, his attitude was much more like that of Franklin Delano Roosevelt with his famous remark that we had nothing to fear but fear itself. The president was not wrong. Fearmongering about the pandemic has been enormously consequential and will inevitably have long-lasting negative effects in terms of public trust and confidence. But the media preferred a narrative of fear, and they went with that because it also served the interests of Democratic politicians who thought it made President Trump look bad, as if his optimism was somehow blameworthy. I'll take his optimism every day. That is classic Americanism.

To say the obvious, the vice president is a very different man from the president. What they share is an underappreciated intellect, a capability to handle enormous loads of work, and a strong appreciation for loyalty. It was an honor to work for them both.

Mike Pence is the grandson of an Irish immigrant, as I am. My grandfather on my mother's side came from County Mayo in Ireland, passed through Ellis Island in the early 1900s, and rose to be an exceptionally successful builder in San Francisco, California. His four daughters all went to university, and one graduated from Stanford Medical School in the late 1930s. Pence is also the son of a combat veteran decorated for heroism in the Korean War. His son is a United States Marine Corps fighter pilot, and a son-in-law is a navy fighter pilot. His family bleeds service to nation.

To me, Pence was "Ice," calm, cool, utterly professional, content to let Trump have center stage, reserving his advice and recommendations to private meetings. Pence never raised his voice, never uttered a profanity, was always quick to offer a pat on the back (even when we needed a boot in the behind), and served the president extremely well as his point man on China, the COVID-19 pandemic, and the creation of a new branch of the military: Space Force. President Trump gave him a large portfolio because Pence was able, reliable, and dutiful. He was the perfect vice president, and would be, in my estimation, a superb president, a man truly worthy of the people's trust.

Near the end of President Trump's administration, Ivanka Trump turned to me in an Oval Office meeting and said, "Mike Pence is a good man."

I could only say, "Yes, he is."

■ ■ ■

On Friday, 27 December 2019, an Iranian-backed proxy group in Iraq, Kata'ib Hezbollah, launched a missile attack on an allied air base, K-1, in northern Iraq near the Kurdish city of Erbil. More than thirty missiles were fired and a naturalized U.S. citizen contractor working for Valiant, an American corporation, was killed. Four U.S. soldiers were injured.

A strike by thirty missiles was more than a small, random, harassing attack. It was a deliberate large-scale strike. On several occasions we had publicly said that if Americans were killed by the Iranians, or by their proxies, we would hold Iran responsible. We could not have been clearer. But Iran and its supporting militias in Iraq had grown increasingly arrogant. They did not believe we were serious. They were wrong. A "red line" for this administration had been crossed.

The pro-Iranian proxy groups in Iraq took their guidance from the Iranian Islamic Revolutionary Guards Corps Quds Force led by Qasem Soleimani. Since 1998, Quds Force had been the Iranian military organization responsible for extraterritorial, unconventional, terrorist, and clandestine operations. Soleimani was a charismatic leader and personally directed all Iranian external operations, which meant that any attacks on American personnel in the region could be traced back to him.

President Obama had declared him a terrorist in 2011, and he was a key supplier of "explosively formed penetrator" IEDs (improvised explosive devices) powerful enough to destroy armored wheeled vehicles and tanks. These were the most deadly and destructive IEDs in Iraq, killing more than four hundred Americans. American blood was already on Soleimani's hands, and now there was no doubt he was behind the attack on K-1. Soleimani did not realize that President Trump was ready to escalate any confrontation that Soleimani started.

The president was at Mar-a-Lago and was briefed by General Mark Milley, chairman of the Joint Chiefs, via a secure teleconference in the Situation Room, where the vice president and I were also present.

Gen. Milley recommended air strikes against several Iranian surrogate groups. The process was simple: one briefing, recommendation given, approved by the president, done. Two days later, U.S. Air Force F-15s hit five different Iranian proxy targets in Syria and Iraq.

Again, the president had been decisive, which was good, but I thought Milley's recommendation, which the president had approved, was too conservative. We had often discussed scenarios about how we should respond to Iranian aggression. I repeatedly commented that "proportional" tit-for-tat attacks were ineffective, because we invariably pulled our punches, and our enemies could calculate that we would never hurt them as much as they annoyed, harassed, or embarrassed us. I said that if the Iranians hit us, we should hit them harder, to make sure they "got it." You hit one of our ships, you lose your entire navy. You hit an airfield, you lose all of your airfields. You kill an American and your leadership is at risk. I argued that escalating like this would obviously change the enemy's calculation, and we would be far more likely to achieve the sort of deterrence we wanted.

I knew the president agreed with my approach, but he always weighed very heavily the advice he received from the Pentagon. Inevitably, the Pentagon's leadership had reservations about escalation; they always argued for a "proportional response." They were trained to think in terms of minimal use of force, and, whenever possible, ignoring provocations.

I understood why my old friend Mark Milley gave the president the advice he did—advice with merit and the authority of Pentagon strategists and analysts behind it. But I knew that, given his druthers, President Trump agreed that the best deterrence comes when an opponent thinks you will hit him three times harder than he hit you. After testing Milley's advice at the first Iranian provocation, I assumed he might follow mine if the Iranians struck again.

In the event, the Iranians responded to our proportional response by testing us. Soleimani ordered Iranian-backed Popular Mobilization Forces to strike at U.S. bases and other American targets.

Not long after five o'clock in the morning on 31 December 2019, my government-issued cell phone rang. It was the watch chief in the White House Situation Room. He asked me to call back on my secure phone.

I called in to the Situation Room and he told me, "Our embassy in Baghdad is under attack." Protesters were attempting to enter the compound and had already breached the outer reception areas. Embassy staff were destroying classified documents in the expectation that embassy security could be breached.

The president was at Mar-a-Lago. His national security adviser was in California. The White House chief of staff was in South Carolina. I was in Arlington, minutes away from the White House. Vice President Pence was at his official residence. His chief of staff, Marc Short, was on a family vacation in Florida. But in short order, we were all connected by phone, and with the help of the Situation Room, I was able to convene a secure conference call with the president, the vice president, the national security adviser, the secretary of defense, and the chairman of the Joint Chiefs.

We briefed the president on events in Baghdad. His response was clear and direct. "The embassy will be secured. Send reinforcements immediately. We are not leaving the embassy. We will not have a repeat of Benghazi," he said, referring to the 2012 incident at our diplomatic compound in Libya where our ambassador, J. Christopher Stephens, had been murdered.

I went into the White House complex and made the Situation Room my home for the next several hours. I called the vice president, but I shouldn't have bothered, because almost as soon as I did, Mike Pence walked into the Situation Room.

Secretary of Defense Mark Esper and General Milley put the president's directives into action immediately. Army AH-64 Apache gunships were ordered into the air to cover the embassy. Marine reinforcements were flown into the embassy grounds on V-22 Osprey tiltrotor aircraft. A squadron of elite army Special Forces was ordered in from Fort Bragg. An American special operations unit working with the Kurds near Erbil was put on alert, as were the eight hundred paratroopers of the army's 82nd Airborne Division Ready Force.

Decision-making at all levels was confident, rapid, and clear. The president's guidance was direct and forceful. The vice president was the point man of the Situation Room.

Later in the day, General Milley looked over to me and said, "Well, we now have three times as many soldiers in the embassy as we had at the Alamo."

I looked across the table and smiled. "Mark, you do remember, we lost the Alamo." As the day progressed, however, the protests at the embassy settled down and the "protesters" took a step back.

But our response had barely begun.

We had highly reliable intelligence reports affirming that our chief enemy here was Soleimani. We had always considered him a legitimate target because he was a sponsor for terrorism and was directly responsible for the deaths and maiming of hundreds of Americans.

The Iranians had crossed our "red line" by killing an American and reinforced their folly by attacking our embassy in Baghdad.

We would respond. And this time our response would be disproportional. We jumped up the escalation ladder. Our answer would be unambiguous. Our target would be Soleimani.

The question was: Would he be traveling, as our intelligence reports indicated, and as he normally did, moving freely around the Middle East to supervise his proxy forces? Or would he being lying low, fearful that we might respond? Most of the president's advisers believed that given our forceful response to events at the embassy, Soleimani would not travel; he would wait to see if that was the extent of our military response. I disagreed. I said, "He will travel—and his arrogance will kill him."

Gina Haspel, the director of the CIA, supported aggressive action, saying, "The risk of doing nothing is greater than the risk of doing something."

We soon had information that Soleimani indeed thought he had nothing to fear. He was taking no extra security precautions. He did not believe we would do anything more than we had, and was pursuing his normal course of travel. He badly misjudged the forty-fifth president of the United States.

Early in the morning of 3 January 2020, deplaning from a commercial flight in Baghdad, Soleimani was met by the Iraqi leader of the Iranian-backed Popular Mobilization Forces, Abu Mahdi al-Muhandis. Their plan was to drive to a safe location to plan future attacks against the United States. As they departed down the airport perimeter road, U.S. drones with Hellfire missiles struck.

We knew the Iranians would be shocked. We knew they would feel compelled to respond. Gina said, "It may be ugly, so buckle up." No one pushed back at me this time when I said we should not be bound by a traditional proportional escalation. We should be clear that we would exact a disproportionately heavy price for any Iranian action against us. Pompeo relayed that message to leaders of several nations that had diplomatic relations with Iran.

We waited. Early on the afternoon of Tuesday, 7 January 2020, I was standing with the president in the Cabinet Room when National Security Adviser Robert O'Brien came in and said we needed to go to the Situation Room. Vice President Pence, Secretary of State Mike Pompeo, Secretary of Defense Mark Esper, Chairman of the Joint Chiefs General Milley, and White House chief of staff Mick Mulvaney were already there. Pompeo said we had received information from both Russian and Swiss governments (the Swiss acted as intermediaries for us with Iran) that the Iranians intended to make a limited strike, not targeting American personnel, and that would be the end of it. In other words, the Iranians were looking to save face, but stop the escalation. It was apparent our attack on Soleimani had totally changed their thinking; they now knew they could not attack us and suffer only minimal responses. This president would forcibly defend American lives.

The Iranians sent sixteen missiles against two targets, al-Asad Air Base in Iraq and Erbil in Iraq's Kurdish zone. Twelve hit their targets while four broke up in flight. We waited. Nothing more followed. The messages we received from the Russians and the Swiss were correct. The Iranian response was limited. We turned to the president. He went around the room asking our thoughts of what we should do. When he got to me, I said, "Do nothing. They sent us a clear message. They want this to end." Some in the room argued otherwise. I told them to watch the footage and note where the Iranian short-range ballistic missiles had hit. If the Iranians had wanted to hit something besides dirt and unoccupied hangars, their guided missiles—which can be accurate to around twelve meters—would have done just that. They sent us a signal, it was "one and done." Some were not convinced and believed we were just "lucky." I strongly disagreed. The president, his arms crossed, listened. After all of us had our say, the president had his: "We're done." He left the Situation Room, and the Iranian "crisis" was over—and it was a win for us. The killing of Soleimani sent shock waves throughout the region. It was a bold and daring strike. The supreme leader of Iran, Ayatollah Khamenei, was stunned and wept at Soleimani's funeral. Prime Minister Netanyahu of Israel later compared our strike to taking "the arm off the tiger." When Joe Biden asked if he would have approved the strike, he said, "No."

But the results of our strike vindicated its wisdom. The Iranians and their Quds Force went quiet. Malign activity from Iran dramatically decreased. And no more Americans were killed by Iranians.

CHAPTER FOURTEEN

Impeachment for Nothing

Once the Mueller investigation was over, the general feeling in the White House was that at last we were done with all the hysterical accusations, harassment, and distractions of the Russia hoax. We had a full plate of policy issues to deal with. It was relief to dispense with the otherwise near-endless, ridiculous "Russia-Russia-Russia" allegations that had driven the media and the "resistance" mad.

I should have known better. I should have known that the anti-Trump forces would need a new obsession to pursue. I never imagined, however, that a phone call between President Trump and President Volodymyr Zelensky of Ukraine would be an issue—and I was on that call.

On the hierarchy of foreign policy issues we faced, our policy with Ukraine ranked well below China, international trade, North Korea, Iran, the Middle East, and NATO. To the president, who felt strongly that our European allies should do more for their own defense and take the lead on European issues, the conflict between Ukraine and Russia was a largely European issue. During the first three years of the Trump presidency, Ukraine policy was rarely a topic of conversation among those of us involved in White House analysis of foreign policy and defense issues.

In 2014, during the Obama-Biden administration, Congress had passed the Ukraine Freedom Support Act in response to the Russian annexation of Crimea from Ukraine. It authorized the administration to impose modest sanctions on Russia and offer modest assistance to Ukraine. Still, the Obama administration had little interest in defending Ukraine or in confronting Russia. It regarded Ukrainian issues as a foreign policy sideshow. Ukrainian issues were low on our foreign policy priorities list, too, but we nevertheless took the intent of the Ukraine Freedom Support Act much more seriously than the Obama administration had.

Since 2014, Ukraine had received more than $1.5 billion in American aid, courtesy of our taxpayers. Unlike the Obama administration, which had provided the Ukrainians with blankets, heaters, and armored vehicles, we provided the Ukrainian military with advanced weaponry. Ukraine acknowledged this was critical to its defense efforts because the European Union would only provide "macro-economic stabilization" money, which didn't do much to stave off the Russians.

President Trump was a consistent advocate for measuring all our foreign aid expenditures by how they benefited American interests. In Ukraine, we judged that our military assistance was effectively helping to protect a friendly country. Still, we knew there were problems with Ukrainian corruption.

President Trump was a jealous guardian of taxpayer funds. He was keenly aware that the United States was deeply in debt. He never forgot that the money we were spending was the American people's money. He wanted proof that their money was spent wisely. He was always interested in cutting unnecessary overseas expenditures to save money; he preferred we look after domestic priorities, like infrastructure, rather than spending money overseas.

The president asked the Office of Management and Budget to evaluate foreign aid expenditures, and where there were concerns about waste or corruption, he wanted aid to be put on hold until the concerns were addressed. Our aid to Ukraine was part of that study and the National Security Council was fully aware of it.

We had no reason to believe that the 2019 Ukrainian election would see a change in government. In fact, we had every reason to believe that the incumbent Ukrainian president, Petro Poroshenko, would win re-election. Poroshenko was an experienced politician, first elected to the country's legislature in 1998, and was a very wealthy man (to his critics he was one of the country's "oligarchs"). His chief opponent was a candidate who had no previous political experience save for a popular Ukrainian television show, *Servant of the People*, on which he appeared as a political figure. With life imitating art (and some thought America's own 2016 election), television star Volodymyr Zelensky handily defeated veteran politician Poroshenko. One of Zelensky's key campaign tenets was defeating political corruption.

A day after Zelensky's landslide win, President Trump called from Air Force One to congratulate him. During the very cordial discussion, Zelensky invited President Trump to attend his inaugural. The president thanked Zelensky for the invitation, but was noncommittal about attending himself, though he promised that "at a minimum we will have a great representative." Two days later, Vice President Pence called to congratulate Zelensky and said, "President Trump has asked me to attend your inauguration, depending on the date" (which was as yet uncertain, because it was to be determined by Ukraine's parliament, the Rada). On both calls, neither Joe Biden nor Burisma, the Ukrainian energy company that had appointed his son, Hunter Biden, to its board, was mentioned.

As a national security adviser, I was on both calls. I gave our ambassador to Ukraine the best travel dates for the vice president (so that Vice President Pence and President Trump would not be outside the country at the same time).

On 16 May 2019 we were told the inauguration was set for 20 May. That date did not work for the vice president, so the United States was represented by Secretary of Energy Rick Perry and U.S. senator Ron Johnson, a Republican from Wisconsin who was a strong supporter of the president and the chairman of the Senate Committee on Homeland Security and Governmental Affairs. On their return, they briefed the president on their meetings with Zelensky. I was in the Oval Office with them during the discussions. Perry and Johnson were effusive in their praise of the new Ukrainian president. There was no discussion of withholding military aid.

On 25 July 2019, President Trump called President Zelensky. Trump was scheduled for a European trip in August and looked forward to meeting the new Ukrainian president. The call was a typical unstructured one during which President Trump discussed whatever was on his mind. I was present for almost every call President Trump had with a head of state. This time, I was in the White House Situation Room with my European specialist, Jennifer Williams, and a small National Security Council team. There was nothing unusual about the call. Did President Trump mention Joe Biden and Hunter Biden? Yes, but what the president stated were facts: "There's a lot of talk about Biden's son, that Biden stopped the prosecution, and a lot of people want to find out about that so whatever you can do with the Attorney General would be great. Biden went around bragging that he stopped the prosecution so if you can look into it…it sounds horrible to me." Corruption was a serious issue in Ukraine—it was, after all, one of the leading reasons Zelensky had been elected president—and Trump had made a particular point that American foreign aid should not be funneled into the hands of oligarchs or be siphoned off by corrupt officials. It's also worth remembering that not only was Joe Biden a private citizen in July 2019, but the Democratic primary season had not kicked off yet. At the time, I thought the call utterly unremarkable. In fact, it was quickly forgotten because of other pressing issues—one of which included a Category Five hurricane, Dorian, which canceled the president's European trip.

On 29 August, the director of the Federal Emergency Management Agency (FEMA) briefed the president and vice president on Hurricane

Dorian, which was headed for Florida's eastern coast. Category Five hurricanes are the highest rated and most dangerous, and all indications were that Dorian's impact on Florida could be severe. All the president's advisers in that Oval Office meeting told the president that he should not travel overseas with a hurricane of this magnitude pending. Everyone remembered Hurricane Andrew in 1992 and the damage Florida had sustained. I had traveled to the Florida Panhandle with the vice president to see the damage after Hurricane Michael, another Category Five, that had hit Tyndall Air Force Base in 2018. I could attest to what kind of damage could happen. Only three Category Five hurricanes were known to have hit Florida previously: Michael, Andrew, and the Labor Day hurricane of 1935. The two most recent were devastating. The president might be needed to help direct the federal government's emergency response.

The president turned to the vice president. "Mike, can you do the trip to Europe?"

The vice president's response was immediate: "Yes." We were fortunate to have the presidential advance team already on the ground in Poland along with National Security Adviser John Bolton; all we had to do was call an audible and plug the vice president into the president's travel schedule. We were in the air on 31 August 2019 and arrived in Warsaw on 1 September for a ceremony marking the eightieth anniversary of the start of World War II. After the ceremony we were scheduled for a bilateral meeting with President Zelensky.

Usually, head of state bilateral meetings are restricted in size, four or five per side at the most. This time the number was doubled, and among those attending with us were Secretary of Energy Rick Perry and the Ukrainian defense minister. Pence and Zelensky sat side by side at the head of the table and engaged in a very warm discussion. One of the tasks given to Pence by President Trump was to "get a sense of the guy." We were all impressed. Personable, sincere, with a high level of energy…my first thought was that President Zelensky and President Trump would get along very well together.

Once the preliminaries were over, Zelensky brought up the issue of financial aid. Bolton had met with Zelensky earlier and, saying the obvious, had warned us this was coming. Pence was noncommittal about increasing American aid, because of President's Trump well-known desire to review American aid expenditures to ensure that we weren't wasting tax dollars. You could feel the air go out of the room on the Ukrainian side; this was their key issue—securing more American aid—and they were obviously disappointed. Zelensky said that his government regarded American support as vital; it was much more important to Ukraine than the support of any country in the European Union. Vice President Pence understood, and congratulated Zelensky on his anti-corruption reforms. The vice president was cordial, but did not commit the United States to any additional expenditures. Not once during the meeting was there any discussion of Joe Biden, Hunter Biden, or Burisma. I had prepared talking points for the vice president and we had discussed them before the meeting. The Bidens and Burisma did not figure at all in those talking points or in our discussions. When the vice president reboarded Air Force Two and called President Trump to tell him about the meeting with Zelensky, Biden was not brought up; Burisma was not brought up. On 11 September 2019, the congressionally mandated aid for Ukraine was released. I was in on every meeting and every discussion regarding Zelensky and aid for Ukraine. Never once was there any talk of a quid pro quo—that if Zelensky did something for us, then we would release that aid. The aid was dispensed after a review to ensure the funds were being properly allocated. None of us thought much about it until it was reported that there was a whistleblower's complaint. The complaint alleged that during his call with Zelensky, President Trump had tried to manipulate a foreign leader for domestic political purposes.

As with the earlier Russia investigation, all of us knew that the allegations were groundless, and the president, confident that he had nothing to hide, immediately suggested that we release the transcript of his call with Zelensky. Secretary of State Mike Pompeo didn't like the idea of setting a precedent for a president's release of transcripts of his calls with foreign leaders, but otherwise none of us had any objections to making the call public.

On 25 September 2019, the transcript of the call was released. The president wanted the transcript released and released it voluntarily; indeed, he wanted to be utterly transparent to show how wrong the so-called whistleblower was. He, like the rest of us, saw nothing wrong with the call. He called it "totally appropriate" and "perfect." What we misjudged was not the actual call, not the reality of the events, not the facts, but the utter vindictiveness of the Democrats who still refused to accept President Trump as a legitimate president, and an inflamed media that seemed interested in nothing more substantive than hysteria and left-wing conspiracy theories. They were surely not interested in the truth.

The day before the transcript's release, House Speaker Nancy Pelosi initiated an official impeachment inquiry based on the whistleblower complaint. The fact that Pelosi had not even waited for the transcript's release, which she knew was coming, told us all we needed to know about the motivations for the inquiry. Also telling was that the impeachment inquiry was sent to the highly partisan House Intelligence Committee (rather than the House Judiciary Committee, which had overseen the Mueller investigation). The House Intelligence Committee was chaired by Adam Schiff, for whom the pursuit of the Russian collusion hoax, remained—even after the Mueller report—an obsession. And in the end, what was achieved? An impeachment in the House and acquittal in the Senate. The bar for impeachment was not lowered, it was eliminated. Impeachment was an obsession that distracted Congress from much more serious issues, real ones, ones that would have enormous consequences for America's immediate future.

CHAPTER FIFTEEN

The Wuhan Pandemic

I would venture that on New Year's Day 2020, most Americans would not have been able to find Wuhan, China, on a map. But the novel coronavirus (COVID-19) that originated there became a global health crisis and the defining issue of 2020. The pandemic led to unprecedent "lockdowns" in free countries; political, cultural, and economic upheaval; and more than three million deaths worldwide.

When the virus hit, overall unemployment in the United States was at 3.5 percent, a fifty-year low; the jobless rates for Asian Americans and adult women were even lower, at 2.5 percent and 3.1 percent respectively; black and Hispanic unemployment rates were at record lows. The economy was booming. In February 2020, a Gallup study reported that nine in ten Americans were satisfied with the way things were going in their personal lives. The previous high for that question was 88 percent in 1983. Yet just months later, a *Wall Street Journal* article by Gerald Seib noted, "The country is heading towards a coronavirus election."

In the end, despite horrific numbers of deaths related to the virus, we would eventually succeed in defeating it, primarily through the historic development and use of vaccines. It will take time for an honest accounting, but it is undeniable that the Trump administration's extraordinary Operation Warp Speed put America on the road to recovery and COVID-19 on the road to defeat, with the development of not one, not two, but three protective vaccines within one year—an unheard of, historic accomplishment. That needs to be part of the story. For an administration that was allegedly "anti-science," we helped achieve one of the great medical breakthroughs of our time. As many publicly said, it was a miracle. But it was a miracle because the administration leaned into it, hard.

The Trump administration was never "anti-science" and the people who make that charge are obviously more interested in name-calling than facts. As it was a novel coronavirus, a lot of the "science" around COVID-19 was a work in progress. The president was extremely attentive to the medical advice he was given—and that advice kept changing. In February 2020, Drs. Anthony Fauci (director of the National Institute of Allergy and Infectious Diseases), H. Clifford Lane (deputy director for Clinical Research and Special Projects at the NIAID), and Robert Redfield (director of the Centers for Disease Control and Prevention) published an article in the *New England Journal of Medicine* titled "Covid-19—Navigating the Uncharted." Their unremarkable conclusion was that "The Covid-19 outbreak is a stark reminder of the ongoing challenge of emerging and reemerging infectious pathogens and the need for constant surveillance, prompt diagnosis, and robust research to understand the basic biology of new organisms and our susceptibilities to them, as well as to develop effective countermeasures." To say the least, there was a lot we didn't know.

I was on the front lines of the battle against the coronavirus every single day as a member of the vice president's coronavirus task force. It was an enormous fight with historic consequences. As Fauci said in October 2020, "This is an outbreak of historic proportions, the likes of which we have not seen in 102 years."

In the war against the coronavirus, I saw many reasonable people succumb to fear. They let themselves get carried away by a media more interested in scaremongering than in facts, in presumed partisan polit-ical gain for the Democrats than in serving the American people. It was stunning to me that the president's emotional resilience, his insistence on pushing through difficulties, his optimism, his desire to restore the "old normal" as swiftly as possible so that people could reclaim their lives, go back to work, return their kids to school, regain the freedoms their state and local governments had denied them, was egregiously misrepresented as heartlessness or obliviousness when a better descrip-tion would have been courage, leadership, and compassion. President Trump put America's medical industry on a wartime footing. He moved swiftly to protect the American people (sometimes more swiftly than his advisers recommended, as in his China travel ban) and was quick to offer federal assistance to states whenever he could, with ventilators, with temporary hospitals (including both navy hospital ships), and with steadily improving tests and the development and use of therapeutics like remdesivir and Regeneron. I do not see how he could have done anything more than he did.

We received reports in late December 2019 of a localized outbreak of a new respiratory virus around the Chinese city of Wuhan. Wuhan, a city of more than eleven million people, sits deep inland and is the most populous city in central China. A traditional manufacturing hub, its economic tentacles stretch throughout the world.

Wuhan is also the site of China's first biosafety level four (BSL-4) laboratory, the Wuhan Institute of Virology. It was known as an active institute for the study of coronaviruses and "gain of function" research, which increases the lethality and transmission of pathogens, like the novel coronavirus, for experimental purposes. BSL-4 laboratories are facilities with the highest level of biocontainment capability. Because of that, dangerous pathogens can be studied in them, and it remains a serious possibility that the virus causing COVID-19 was inadvertently released from the Wuhan Institute of Virology. No less an authority than CDC's Dr. Robert Redfield, a virologist, said in March 2021, "I am of the point of view that I still think the most likely etiology of this pathogen in Wuhan was from a laboratory, you know, escaped. . . . It's not unusual for respiratory pathogens that are being worked on in the laboratory to infect the laboratory worker." During my time with the task force, I became a believer in the possibility and probability that the pandemic stemmed from an inadvertent release of an experimental coronavirus from the Wuhan lab. It was a theory that was met by early and swift derision from Dr. Anthony Fauci, who, it later turned out, had overseen taxpayer money going to the Wuhan lab, and had an obvious interest in denying that the coronavirus had escaped from there. Fauci should have told Vice President Pence about his involvement with funding the Wuhan lab and recused himself from the ensuing discussion. He did neither. Even worse, he publicly discounted any theory of a lab release, and the press followed his lead. Only later would the media start to report on the likely possibility of a Wuhan lab leak. Fauci's behavior was egregious.

In early January 2020, the Atlanta-based Centers for Disease Control observed and reported a significant viral outbreak in China. Clusters of sickness in Wuhan indicated it was caused by a different strain of coronavirus than we had observed in previous outbreaks.

Within a few days we received a CDC follow-on report that the virus was expanding rapidly in Wuhan and the surrounding province of Hubei. We also noted an unusually rapid and aggressive reaction from the Chinese government. By 23 January 2020, Wuhan, a city five times the size of London, was being shut down and quarantined by military and police with public transportation closed and severe travel restrictions imposed. Hundreds of thousands had fled the city before the restrictions fell into place. Prefabricated hospitals went up overnight. Eventually, Hubei province was put under quarantine—the equivalent of the United States government quarantining California, Oregon, and Washington. One thing we noted was that the shockingly aggressive Chinese response seemed all out of proportion to Chinese reporting on the disease, which denied that the novel coronavirus was a serious threat. This was the start of a long and continuing pattern of Chinese lies and obfuscations as we tried to learn more about the virus.

Health and Human Services Secretary Alex Azar alerted us that China was refusing entry to our investigative research teams from the CDC. This was a first, as international health authorities are generally among the most cooperative international agencies. The World Health Organization, however, was still not raising alarms. As late as 14 January 2020, it was reporting no cases of human-to-human transmission.

The Chinese New Year was on 25 January 2020, and January is the busiest holiday travel season for Chinese citizens. Hundreds of thousands of expatriate Chinese returned to China for the New Year celebrations and then flew to New York and Milan and even Snohomish, Washington. Global passenger traffic remained unrestricted. There were no medical checks, no outward concerns, no official communication from China that there was anything we should worry about. In 2018, the United States had almost three million visitors from China. The *New York Times* estimated that in the first three months of 2020, 430,000 people had traveled from China to the United States. Key to putting that figure in context is that President Trump imposed a travel ban on China on 31 January.

Until President Trump's travel ban, the coronavirus was hardly a national issue at all. It certainly played no part in the vice president's next scheduled overseas trip to Israel and Europe. While the American "patient zero" (a U.S. citizen from Snohomish who had visited his extended family in Wuhan for Chinese New Year) was being tested and diagnosed, the vice president was flying from Joint Base Andrews aboard Air Force Two bound for Jerusalem. There he was to give a speech at the Yad Vashem Holocaust memorial, commemorating the seventy-fifth anniversary of the liberation of Auschwitz, as well as International Remembrance Day, when the world marks the tragedy of the Holocaust. The vice president was joined by dozens of world leaders, including the United Kingdom's Prince Charles, French president Emmanuel Macron, and Russian president Vladimir Putin. In every conversation among these leaders where I was present, no one mentioned the coronavirus—not once.

Instead, our thoughts were entirely on the unspeakable atrocity that was the Holocaust. On an earlier trip to Poland, the vice president and I had traveled to Auschwitz and walked the eerily silent grounds of the former Nazi concentration and extermination camp. That experience made a deep impact on all of us who were there. Standing at the very spot where Jews, many of them children, were unloaded from railroad cars and then murdered in gas chambers made me pause. For a few minutes I just stood and took in the landscape, marking the spot where families were separated and sent to their deaths—more than a million people, murdered for simply having Jewish blood. I commented to the vice president as we reboarded Air Force Two that afternoon, "How could God allow this to happen?" The vice president said something I will always remember: "It wasn't God, it was man."

Our trip to Jerusalem included a visit to our new American embassy. Many presidents before Trump had said, pro forma, that they favored moving the American embassy to Jerusalem and recognizing Jerusalem as Israel's capital (such a move was authorized by Congress in 1995), but none had ever done it. Trump did—another promise kept and another reason for the president's popularity in Israel and with Israeli prime minister Benjamin Netanyahu. The new embassy officially opened in May 2018 on the seventieth anniversary of the creation of the modern state of Israel. Previous presidents had shied away from the move because they thought the Arab nations would find it provocative, the so-called "Arab Street" might explode in violence, and that it might spark another Palestinian intifada. None of that happened because President Trump dramatically changed the environment in the Middle East. He successfully rallied states like Saudi Arabia to recognize that Iran, not Israel, was the chief threat to their security. Indeed, he helped Arab states recognize that Israel could be a valuable ally against Iranian regional ambitions. I was amused to hear, in April 2020, presidential candidate Joe Biden declare that the American embassy "should not have been moved" from Tel Aviv to Jerusalem, but that he would keep it in Jerusalem if elected. Now that was a politician speaking!

As we sat in the U.S. ambassador's office that evening with the Israeli prime minister, his national security adviser, Meir Ben-Shabbat, and our respective ambassadors, the talks were relaxed and cordial. The discussion was centered on the progress being made for peace between the Arabs and the Israelis, the political situation in Iran, and our recent strike on Soleimani. The vice president was very interested in what the Israelis thought about the strike and how they assessed the reaction of their Arab neighbors. Netanyahu was unequivocal: "The region is safer because of what you did. The Iranians are on their heels." One thing we did not discuss: the coronavirus.

Our next stop was Italy. The vice president and I reviewed his schedule, including his audience with the pope (Mike Pence is a former Catholic) and meeting with the president and prime minister of Italy. We monitored the ongoing Senate impeachment trial of Donald Trump. We never discussed the coronavirus.

At the Vatican, Vice President Pence was treated as a head of state and enjoyed an unusually long one-on-one meeting with the pope. Afterward, a small group was offered a chance to meet Pope Francis. I was fortunate to be part of this group and asked Pope Francis to bless a handful of rosaries I had brought with me. Meeting him was an extraordinary experience; shaking hands with him, I immediately felt I was in the presence of a man of spiritual authority. His eyes seem to pierce your soul, to see through to your essence, but in a kind, gentle, and forgiving way.

Later that afternoon, we headed to the presidential palace and meetings with Italian prime minister Giuseppe Conte and president Sergio Mattarella. The chief items of discussion were Italy's reluctance to meet its obligations to NATO and its struggles with mass immigration. Here too, the coronavirus never came up, though Italy would soon dominate world headlines with its COVID-19 crisis.

That evening we were hosted at dinner by our ambassador to the Vatican, Callista Gingrich, and her husband, Newt Gingrich, former Speaker of the House. They were very keen to discuss political developments in the United States, and possible future political trends, but one thing that none of us foresaw—indeed, that none of us mentioned even in passing—was a COVID-19 pandemic.

The next day, we flew home on Air Force Two and our attention was riveted to the impeachment trial. Because I had been on the president's phone call with Ukrainian president Zelensky, my name came up, though ultimately in an inconsequential way. The president's defense team did a good job, I thought, but I also thought they should not have had to do this job at all. None of us should have been distracted from our duties by this politically motivated, groundless impeachment. It had nothing substantive to do with our Ukrainian policy (except to expose a body of bureaucrats who were opposed to it) or to any sort of misconduct (since, as the president constantly—and correctly—asserted, he had done nothing wrong). This entire farce was nothing more than a Democrat-led effort to harass the president and harm his chances for reelection.

Returning from the trip, I called Bob Redfield at the CDC. Though the coronavirus had not figured in any of our overseas discussions, I had made it part of my portfolio to keep tabs on the issue. Redfield told me we had five confirmed coronavirus cases in the United States. All of the infected individuals had traveled to China for the Chinese New Year celebrations. Five cases in a country of 350 million people did not raise any pandemic alarm bells.

What did keep me interested was this: COVID-19 seemed to be, for now, a nearly entirely Chinese problem. The Chinese government continued to insist, whenever it communicated any information at all, that there was no medical crisis in the offing. But their observed response still raised questions. A country does not involve its military internally and lock down a major city unless something out of the ordinary is happening. Of course, we did not know precisely what was happening, but we knew enough to be suspicious of the Chinese government's tight-lipped reassurances that this was a matter of only local concern.

That suspicion led to the creation of a small coronavirus task force. White House chief of staff Mick Mulvaney and Health and Human

Services Secretary Alex Azar were co-chairs of a daily meeting in the White House Situation Room to track what the Chinese were doing. Bob Redfield also attended, and I represented the vice president's office.

In some ways, we were much better prepared than the administration's critics would acknowledge. Not only did we discuss possible pandemic scenarios, but only a year before the National Security Council had worked with Secretary Azar, the leaders of other federal departments, and state governments to map out a "what if" plan based on the possibility of a pandemic respiratory virus coming from China. We ran a comprehensive tabletop exercise called Crimson Contagion. The Crimson Contagion wargame, if you want to call it that, was carried out from January to August 2019. It made recommendations for how we could better prepare ourselves for a possible pandemic. But enacting those recommendations over the six months between the end of the wargame and our initial suspicions about the novel coronavirus in China would have been more than ambitious, given the many agencies involved. I also reviewed the George W. Bush administration's $7.1 billion plan to protect America from a pandemic. It was a tremendously ambitious plan, well enacted, but never really put to the test—not as we would be. Announced in 2005, much of its infrastructure still existed, but revving it up for an immediate threat would have been a challenge (a challenge that the president ultimately met, in my opinion, with Operation Warp Speed and our other efforts). I also pulled the Obama's administration "playbook" for dealing with a pandemic and found it wanting. It was long on boilerplate and short on recommendations except to look to the World Health Organization for guidance and defer to its recommendations. But from what I could tell, the World Health Organization's information was no better than our own, its record of faulty predictions did not inspire confidence, and there was already a strong sense that it was in China's pocket. The World Health Organization's director-general was Dr. Tedros Adhanom Ghebreyesus. Elected to the post in 2017, he had been China's candidate, and his early advice on the coronavirus seemed to follow Chinese talking points. On 3 February 2020, Tedros opposed such measures as international travel bans, which he said "unnecessarily interfere with international travel and trade," and praised China's president Xi Jinping for his leadership in ensuring that the spread of the virus was "minimal and slow." It would be fair to say that at this point in the looming COVID-19 crisis, the Trump administration was ahead of the World Health Organization in responding to the limited information we had.

All of our intelligence pointed in the same direction. In the words of a late January report from the Defense Intelligence Agency, the virus "was unlikely to move to a pandemic." But we did not sit idly by. We started with health screenings at major airports and tried to funnel every passenger from China to select airports. The idea was to isolate passengers who had a fever or were otherwise symptomatic. This was a standard medical procedure. It was "following the science." But it also proved to be entirely inadequate because no one yet appreciated how many pre-symptomatic carriers there were. In other words, you could be sick and able to infect others but not yet showing obvious signs of illness. We had no information on this from China, even though the Chinese obviously knew much more about it. We eventually had reports that *80 percent* of those infected might be pre-symptomatic or asymptomatic, some never showing any signs of illness.

Americans were in the Wuhan hot zone, and we needed to get them out. The president demanded we protect our people—and he didn't mean in a week, he meant now. We closed our consulate in Wuhan and were determined to evacuate all American citizens as a group in a chartered aircraft.

On 29 January 2020, we airlifted 195 U.S. citizens out of Wuhan. We had them in the air before we even knew where they were going to land or under what quarantine circumstances. We finally settled on California's March Air Reserve Base in Riverside County. We assumed the passengers would be isolated there for three days, but CDC director Bob Redfield gave us new medical guidance, and a quarantine period of fourteen days was imposed. Still, with one exception, our passengers were overjoyed just to be out of Wuhan, even if it meant a fourteen-day quarantine. A federal mandatory quarantine order solved the issue for the one objector.

No sooner had we taken these precautions than we faced the problem of cruise ships, which, we assumed, could become floating petri dishes if their passengers picked up the coronavirus.

In early February, the cruise ship *Diamond Princess*, sailing off the coast of Japan with many American passengers, reported an outbreak of coronavirus cases. The ship docked in Yokohama and was quarantined by the Japanese: no one on, no one off. The State Department worked out an agreement that allowed us to evacuate American passengers who wanted to leave the ship and who would agree to a fourteen-day quarantine stateside. We sent the passengers to Travis Air Force Base, California, and to Lackland Air Force Base in Texas.

It was obvious that we could not keep evacuating American citizens like this. We had, after all, only so many military bases available. We were also well aware that the 1918 Spanish flu had spread rapidly on military bases, and we did not want a repeat of that experience.

The question was how we could contain the virus—still largely confined to China—without much in the way of cooperation from the Chinese. If containment failed, the next step was mitigation. That meant, depending on how contagious the virus was, we might be dealing with something comparable, at the very least, to a flu epidemic of unknown severity.

Meanwhile, we had caught a break. On 11 January 2020, Dr. Yong-Zhen Zhang, a resident at Shanghai's Public Health Clinical Center, had released the genetic code of the virus online. Within hours of the release, the Chinese government closed down Dr. Zhang's laboratory for "rectification"; it would stay shut down for weeks. But our National Institutes of Health (NIH) now had something to study so the search for an effective vaccine could begin. China would continue to claim that there was no sign of human-to-human transmission of the virus until 20 January, when that position became totally untenable as researchers and scientists studied the genetic code and gathered further data.

On 30 January 2020, Vice President Pence, senior members of the coronavirus task force, and key cabinet officials converged on the Oval Office. Vice President Pence carried with him dire information from Drs. Redfield and Fauci. Because of China's lack of transparency about the virus, we were facing many unknowns, but it appeared that asymptomatic cases were high, and the infection rate was alarming. Fauci warned that the infection rate could be even higher than the infection rate for measles. Measles is so contagious that one person can infect 90 percent of the people around him. While no deaths had yet been reported in the United States, extreme caution was warranted.

Vice President Pence and Secretary of State Pompeo wanted to institute a travel ban on China. So did Peter Navarro, an assistant to the president and a China expert. I was all in. But others, including Secretary of the Treasury Steve Mnuchin, were strongly opposed. The contending groups got into a heated discussion in front of the president. Normally, President Trump was open to freewheeling discussions, but he recognized that this one was not constructive. There was no baseline consensus, and we were essentially doing staff work in front of the president, wasting his time. Trump told Pence, with some irritation, "Go into the Cabinet Room and come back in thirty minutes with a recommendation. I just want to keep the American people safe."

The Cabinet Room discussion was no less heated. I looked at my watch and informed the vice president that our requisite thirty minutes was over; we had to make a call. Pence told the group, "Okay, I appreciate all that has been said. The president was clear. The safety of Americans comes first. Our consensus position is to execute a travel ban on China effective this coming weekend."

We returned to the Oval Office and Pence told President Trump that "out of an abundance of caution, we recommend a travel ban." Mnuchin tried to have the last word by telling the president, "I disagree with the decision." So much for consensus. But the president ignored him and told Vice President Pence to make it happen.

On Friday afternoon, 31 January 2020, Health and Human Services Secretary Alex Azar announced the travel ban on China.

Within hours, criticism came our way. Democratic presidential contender Joe Biden attacked the travel ban and accused the president of having a "record of hysteria, xenophobia, and fearmongering." A *New York Times* article said that the president's decision to restrict travel from China was "more of an emotional or political reaction." The *Washington Post* slammed the decision by saying we were "in disregard of World Health Organization recommendations against travel restrictions." That was true, but as I noted, we put less trust in the World Health Organization than did the nation's liberal editorial writers. The WHO disapproved of our action, saying there was "no need" for it, and that it would "unnecessarily interfere with world trade." How many of those who say that the president didn't react quickly enough, and didn't take the looming pandemic seriously enough, remember that it was Joe Biden, the WHO, the *New York Times*, the *Washington Post*, and so many other prominent liberal voices who accused President Trump of *overreacting*? The liberal website Vox, which is supposed to help people "understand the news," tweeted on 31 January 2020, "Is this going to be a deadly pandemic? No." More than a month later, Vox deleted the tweet.

We were buying time and we knew it. Even if some were downplaying the threat, the president's instincts were on overdrive. While he was ever the optimist, and intent on putting a brave face on things, I knew he was more worried than some of his advisers were. As late as 29 February 2020, Tony Fauci told NBC, "Right now, at this moment, there is no need to change anything you are doing on a day-to-day basis. Right now, the risk is low, but this could change."

In late February, there were, according to Drs. Fauci and Redfield, a total of fifty-nine known cases in the United States. In early March, my daughter was to fly to visit us with my two granddaughters. I asked

Dr. Fauci if it was safe and if they should wear masks. The answers were, yes, it was safe, and no, they did not need to wear masks.

But one person on our staff recognized that a dam was about to break. Matt Pottinger had been one of my first hires. He was a China hand. A former Marine, he had also been a *Wall Street Journal* reporter in China during a previous coronavirus outbreak. As the deputy national security adviser, he served on the initial coronavirus task force. Matt told Trump, "Mr. President, this will be the biggest national security crisis of your presidency. The Chinese are lying to the world. They are facing a crisis. They have imposed the equivalent of martial law in Wuhan. What they're doing is unprecedented. We need to be prepared if they don't contain it."

Our travel ban was meant to shore up containment, but Europe had not instituted a travel ban on China. Most senior medical officials, to include the World Health Organization, had argued against travel bans, and foreign governments followed their advice. They shouldn't have done that.

Italy's second most populous city is Milan, with a thriving textile industry and more than twenty thousand Chinese residents. Throughout Italy, there are well over 320,000 Chinese residents. Many traveled to China in January for the Chinese New Year celebrations. Even as the first cases of COVID-19 started to appear, most Italian officials downplayed the threat, with the mayor of Florence even instituting a "Hug a Chinese" program, because he feared that racism was a bigger threat than the coronavirus. In Italy, the first locally transmitted case was confirmed in Milan—and the case numbers escalated rapidly, to the point that Milan's hospitals were getting overwhelmed. Italy has a healthy but aged population, and the virus hit the elderly the hardest. Doctors were making the equivalent of military field hospital decisions, separating out patients who might have a chance of survival from those who likely didn't. The shocking situation in Italy, which got saturation media coverage, gave the world the wake-up call that China had tried to keep muffled.

All previous pandemic plans, including those of the Obama administration, envisioned the secretary of Health and Human Services leading the pandemic response. The president had a different plan. He sensed that we needed more senior leadership, someone who could lead both an interagency effort and coordinate action with the states. Who better than Vice President Pence, a former governor and a former congressman holding the full authoritative backing of the White House? In retrospect, it was an obvious and wise decision—but none of us expected it, because the case numbers in the United States were still very low (under one hundred), and the vice president's in-box had no shortage of work stuffed into it. But the president was ahead of the rest of the administration in sensing—and agreeing with Matt Pottinger—that he was going to face a health crisis exported from China. Trump's style is always to be confident, but he is more than willing to make changes when necessary, and he wanted Pence in charge of our coronavirus response. He wanted his entire administration involved in the effort. He summoned Vice President Pence to the Oval Office. Marc Short and I went with him. Trump told him flatly, "I think you should lead the virus task force."

Pence said, "Yes, Mr. President." And it was done. The president gave us our marching orders: "There is no higher priority than the health and safety of the American people." We now had all the authority we needed.

The initial task force was small, but under the vice president's leadership it expanded. The most visible addition was Dr. Deborah Birx, an expert in infectious disease, who became the vice president's chief de facto medical adviser as the task force coordinator. Birx was a retired U.S. army colonel who had worked at the Walter Reed National Military Medical Center and had a long working relationship with Tony Fauci. Smart, poised, and data driven, Birx was a steady hand during the crisis and, in the beginning, did a good job of being our public face, our media messenger.

Unfortunately, she was displaced as our chief medical spokesperson by Dr. Fauci. Fauci's medical knowledge was never in doubt, though his advice and his judgments were, and he had a penchant for making comments best left to elected officials. He also tended, at times, to be very wrong. He would later say that he was "the skunk at the garden party." At the task force meetings that was true, but it didn't mean he was right. He did our work no favors by injecting himself into politics, and he never seemed to understand that there were more interests and arguments to be weighed than his own. In a task force meeting, I once said to him in frustration: "Tony, you don't understand either the Constitution or federalism. Stay in your lane."

Jared Kushner shared my frustration with Fauci. After another, typically pessimistic comment from Fauci, Kushner said, "You doctors are scaring the shit out of America." By our reckoning, there was no excuse for that. None of us wanted to be unrealistic, but we also saw no reason to deprive people of hope, when we and so many other authorities were working so hard to build hope. COVID-19 was undoubtedly a dangerous disease for many people, it was deadly serious, but it was not a replay of the Spanish Flu pandemic. Fauci, and other experts, sometimes seemed to lack a sense of perspective.

In addition, they were not always straightforward with the facts. In a very public discussion in front of the Washington press corps, Fauci said there was no possibility of a lab-generated release, while making no mention of the NIH's support for the Wuhan Institute of Virology's gain of function research on coronaviruses. Fauci was closely aligned with a group that publicly disputed the lab-release theory, and his comments caused much of the media to disparage it as either racist or xenophobic, when, in fact, the theory was quite credible and even likely to be true.

On a personal level, I liked Tony Fauci, but he reminded me of a medic on a battlefield treating a seriously wounded soldier who asks, "How am I doing?" only to have Fauci take out a cigarette, cut it in half, and say, "Smoke it fast." An optimist he was not.

The media and the Democrats kept screaming that we should "listen to the science" and "listen to the doctors," as if we were shutting them out. But all of us were waiting for data to accumulate. The fact is, we did listen to the scientists, we did listen to the doctors, and their opinions and advice were frequently at odds and sometimes changed unexpectedly. They were often oblivious about the need to balance risks and benefits rather than focus solely on COVID-19. In early February, Bob Redfield told me, "If we can keep it under a thousand deaths, we will be a success." He only missed the mark by several hundred thousand plus. The truth was that not even the doctors and the scientists understood the scope of what we were facing; we were all learning. The lesson for me: doctors are fallible and they should stick to science, not policy.

The president was deeply involved in all of this. He received daily coronavirus briefings (I attended them). He showed constant concern that we do everything we could to protect the American people. Not only were his instincts sound on that, but he understood, better than the experts, that lockdowns and masking and other restrictive measures brought costs as well as benefits and that we needed to offer hope as well as warnings.

On 11 March 2020, the president's meeting with his coronavirus task force lasted well over two hours. He probed his economic and health advisers about what actions they thought were needed. Earlier in the day, the World Health Organization had announced that we were in a global pandemic. The president resolved that it was time to address the nation. He wanted to tell the American people what his advisers had told him—that the current risk to most Americans was low and that special care needed to be taken for the elderly—and to emphasize that we would overcome this challenge.

Here are his remarks. When you read what follows keep in mind the media and Democratic mythology that the president downplayed the virus, that he didn't take it seriously, and that he did nothing about it. That lie cannot be sustained once you read what he actually said on 11 March 2020, once you see what he actually did, and once you appreciate what he achieved with Operation Warp Speed.

> My fellow Americans: Tonight, I want to speak with you about our nation's unprecedented response to the coronavirus

outbreak that started in China and is now spreading throughout the world.

Today, the World Health Organization officially announced that this is a global pandemic.

We have been in frequent contact with our allies, and we are marshaling the full power of the federal government and the private sector to protect the American people.

This is the most aggressive and comprehensive effort to confront a foreign virus in modern history. I am confident that by counting and continuing to take these tough measures, we will significantly reduce the threat to our citizens, and we will ultimately and expeditiously defeat this virus.

From the beginning of time, nations and people have faced unforeseen challenges, including large-scale and very dangerous health threats. This is the way it always was and always will be. It only matters how you respond, and we are responding with great speed and professionalism.

Our team is the best anywhere in the world. At the very start of the outbreak, we instituted sweeping travel restrictions on China and put in place the first federally mandated quarantine in over fifty years. We declared a public health emergency and issued the highest level of travel warning on other countries as the virus spread its horrible infection.

And taking early intense action, we have seen dramatically fewer cases of the virus in the United States than are now present in Europe.

The European Union failed to take the same precautions and restrict travel from China and other hotspots. As a result, a large number of new clusters in the United States were seeded by travelers from Europe.

After consulting with our top government health professionals, I have decided to take several strong but necessary actions to protect the health and well-being of all Americans.

To keep new cases from entering our shores, we will be suspending all travel from Europe to the United States for the next thirty days. The new rules will go into effect Friday at midnight. These restrictions will be adjusted subject to conditions on the ground.

There will be exemptions for Americans who have undergone appropriate screenings, and these prohibitions will not only apply to the tremendous amount of trade and cargo, but various other things as we get approval. Anything coming from Europe to the United States is what we are discussing. These restrictions will also not apply to the United Kingdom.

At the same time, we are monitoring the situation in China and in South Korea. And, as their situation improves, we will reevaluate the restrictions and warnings that are currently in place for a possible early opening.

Earlier this week, I met with the leaders of the health insurance industry who have agreed to waive all copayments for coronavirus treatments, extend insurance coverage to these treatments, and to prevent surprise medical billing.

We are cutting massive amounts of red tape to make antiviral therapies available in record time. These treatments will significantly reduce the impact and reach of the virus.

Additionally, last week, I signed into law an $8.3 billion funding bill to help the CDC and other government agencies fight the virus and support vaccines, treatments, and distribution of medical supplies. Testing and testing capabilities are expanding rapidly, day by day. We are moving very quickly.

For the vast majority of Americans, the risk is very, very low. Young and healthy people can expect to recover fully and quickly if they should get the virus. The highest risk is for the elderly population with underlying health conditions. The elderly population must be very, very careful.

In particular, we are strongly advising that nursing homes for the elderly suspend all medically unnecessary visits. In general, older Americans should also avoid nonessential travel in crowded areas.

My administration is coordinating directly with communities with the largest outbreaks, and we have issued guidance on school closures, social distancing, and reducing large gatherings.

Smart action today will prevent the spread of the virus tomorrow.

Every community faces different risks and it is critical for you to follow the guidelines of your local officials who are working closely with our federal health experts—and they are the best.

For all Americans, it is essential that everyone take extra precautions and practice good hygiene. Each of us has a role to play in defeating this virus. Wash your hands, clean often-used surfaces, cover your face and mouth if you sneeze or cough, and most of all, if you are sick or not feeling well, stay home.

To ensure that working Americans impacted by the virus can stay home without fear of financial hardship, I will soon be taking emergency action, which is unprecedented, to provide financial relief. This will be targeted for workers who are ill, quarantined, or caring for others due to the coronavirus.

I will be asking Congress to take legislative action to extend this relief.

Because of the economic policies that we have put into place over the last three years, we have the greatest economy anywhere in the world, by far.

Our banks and financial institutions are fully capitalized and incredibly strong. Our unemployment is at a historic low.

This vast economic prosperity gives us flexibility, reserves, and resources to handle any threat that comes our way.

This is not a financial crisis; this is just a temporary moment of time that we will overcome together as a nation and as a world.

However, to provide extra support for American workers, families, and businesses, tonight I am announcing the following additional actions: I am instructing the Small Business Administration to exercise available authority to provide capital and liquidity to firms affected by the coronavirus.

Effective immediately, the SBA will begin providing economic loans in affected states and territories. These low-interest loans will help small businesses overcome temporary economic disruptions caused by the virus. To this end, I am asking Congress to increase funding for this program by an additional $50 billion.

Using emergency authority, I will be instructing the Treasury Department to defer tax payments, without interest or penalties, for certain individuals and businesses negatively impacted. This action will provide more than $200 billion of additional liquidity to the economy.

Finally, I am calling on Congress to provide Americans with immediate payroll tax relief. Hopefully they will consider this very strongly.

We are at a critical time in the fight against the virus. We made a lifesaving move with early action on China. Now we must take the same action with Europe. We will not delay. I will never hesitate to take any necessary steps to protect the lives, health, and safety of the American people. I will always put the well-being of America first.

If we are vigilant—and we can reduce the chance of infection, which we will—we will significantly impede the transmission of the virus. The virus will not have a chance against us.

No nation is more prepared or more resilient than the United States. We have the best economy, the most advanced healthcare, and the most talented doctors, scientists, and researchers anywhere in the world.

We are all in this together. We must put politics aside, stop the partisanship, and unify together as one nation and one family.

As history has proven time and time again, Americans always rise to the challenge and overcome adversity.

Our future remains brighter than anyone can imagine. Acting with compassion and love, we will heal the sick, care for those in need, help our fellow citizens, and emerge from this challenge stronger and more unified than ever before.

God bless you, and God bless America. Thank you.

Inevitably, Democratic presidential candidate Joe Biden attacked President Trump's address to the nation, saying, among other things: "Labeling COVID-19 a 'foreign virus' does not displace accountability for the misjudgments that have been taken thus far by the Trump administration." What misjudgments? We were advised daily by the nation's top health experts, and we followed their guidance. But Biden went further, and spun off his criticisms into a political ad that even the *Washington Post* found egregiously deceptive and misleading, awarding it four (out of five) "Pinocchios" for presenting "a false narrative." The *Post* added that "Campaigns must be willing to make their case without resorting to video manipulation." Well, good luck with that. The virus became a political issue in a political year, and the Democrats and the mainstream media (for the most part) could not overcome their prejudices against Donald J. Trump and could not judge our efforts fairly and objectively. I will be frank: I thought this behavior was simply disgraceful. It was political opportunism of the worst kind that misinformed Americans and increased fear.

That misinformation got worse as the press praised New York governor Andrew Cuomo as the anti-Trump: heroic liberal, pro-science, activist governor against the virus. This adulation came even as his state became the worst hit in the country, after he made some very bad decisions about sending COVID-19 patients back to nursing homes and deliberately undercounted deaths. The president, to his credit, ignored all the politics and media partisanship and did everything possible to rush medical help to New York.

Under the Clinton administration, the United States had created a Strategic National Stockpile of critical medical supplies to supplement state and local authorities in medical emergencies involving natural disasters (like hurricanes) or flu epidemics. After the 2009 swine flu pandemic, budget constraints meant that much of the stockpile was not replenished. Even if it had been, the stockpile would not have been ready for a once-in-a-century pandemic of a virus not seen before.

Our response had to be fast, and it was. On 13 March 2020, President Trump declared COVID-19 a national emergency. The administration effort shifted into overdrive. The vice president traveled constantly. He worked with companies like 3M to dramatically increase production of N-95 medical masks. He worked with diagnostic lab companies to ramp up testing. With Admiral Brett Giroir, MD, assistant secretary for health at Health and Human Services, becoming our testing point man, the United States become the world's leader on testing and testing resources. In essence, we went to the private sector and encouraged companies to go onto a wartime footing so that we could fulfill the president's directive to do everything possible to protect the American people from harm. Any slowness we had in getting started was the result of a lack of information—and for that we should blame China, not the Trump administration. Once we started getting more data, we acted on it as fast as anyone could act on it. The president always demanded that we press for more information, that we remove obstructions to progress, and that we light fires under slow-moving bureaucracies. Any narrative that the administration did not act rapidly against the COVID-19 pandemic is absurd. The facts prove otherwise.

We even instituted the equivalent of a domestic Berlin Airlift to acquire additional medical equipment as quickly as possible. Eighty percent of medical personal protective equipment is made overseas. Rather than wait on shipping freighters, with transit times of a month or more, we partnered with UPS and FedEx to use their air assets to bring this equipment stateside. It was called Project Airbridge and slashed the delivery time of critical equipment to two days from twenty-eight-plus by traditional sealift. Over the course of 249 flights, we brought in millions of protective masks, gloves, overgarments, and face shields. The first flight landed on 29 March 2020, bringing eighty tons of supplies to New York and New Jersey.

That same month we sent U.S. Navy hospital ships to assist New York and California. The West Coast–based USNS *Mercy* arrived in Los Angeles harbor and began seeing patients on 29 March while the USNS *Comfort* arrived in New York harbor on 30 March, providing an additional one thousand hospital beds.

On 16 March, the Trump administration had issued a set of medical recommendations for a fifteen-day campaign to slow the spread of the virus. The recommendations were commonsensical and meant to give our hospitals time to gear up for the expected rise in cases. Unfortunately, state and local authorities went far beyond the guidelines, locking down much of the country. Such lockdowns were *not* medical best practice. They were motivated by a combination of fear; panic; bureaucratic overreaction; narrow-minded, single-issue thinking; and the apparent desire of some mayors and governors to take advantage of the situation to wield virtually unlimited power. The full consequences are yet to be wholly measured or appreciated, but they could easily rival or even surpass the deaths and damage caused by the coronavirus itself. Businesses—started or funded by people's life savings—were closed, perhaps forever. Unemployment soared. Children were deprived of school, of a social life. Isolation imposed all sorts of sufferings. Drug abuse and suicides surged. I was haunted by a comment from Dr. Elinor McCance-Katz, assistant secretary of Health and Human Services for mental health and substance abuse. She urged us to keep a sense of perspective and to remember that lives lost to suicide or drug overdose were as important as lives lost to the coronavirus. She warned of the damage done to children through lockdowns and school closings, and how some children, in bad home situations, were now at dramatically greater risk for child abuse. Her comment that "every home is not a safe home" was haunting. CDC director Bob Redfield echoed her comments. "The CDC has never recommended school closings. It is time for schools to open." A year later, many still weren't.

The "fifteen days to slow the spread" announcement coincided with a G7 secure videoconference in the White House Situation Room. The G7 is an international forum consisting of the leadership of the United States, Canada, France, Germany, Italy, Japan, and the United Kingdom. This day it was focused on the coronavirus. The assembled leaders were confident that the virus could be beaten by swift, coordinated action. Prime Minister Shinzo Abe of Japan said his country intended to go forward with the 2020 Tokyo Summer Olympics with spectators in the stands, to which British prime minister Boris Johnson replied, "Hear, hear!" Prime Minister Angela Merkel of Germany was typically more restrained. She told the group, "We are working with a large amount of uncertainty." How right she was.

When the surge of cases hit New York, we offered Governor Cuomo every possible assistance, so much so that much of the assistance we offered—from ventilators to the USNS *Comfort* to the U.S. Army field hospital conversion of New York City's Javits Center—went largely unused. We actually ended up with a surplus of ventilators, especially after doctors decided that they should be used more infrequently. Still, New York became our Milan. The crisis would crest, but the fear would linger. The president understood this, which was one reason why he tried to project optimism (which came to him naturally anyway). He also understood that the only way to get fully and expeditiously out of the crisis was with a vaccine—and the reassurance we would get from it.

The government does not develop or produce vaccines. Private industry does. Vaccines for new viruses normally take years and billions of dollars to develop. If there is no profit incentive and a way for business to recover investment costs, the vaccine development process is slow or nonexistent. Secretary Azar described the process in detail to the president and vice president. He knew it well from his days as the president of Lilly USA, the American division of the Eli Lilly pharmaceutical company.

President Trump is a businessman. He got it. The only way to speed a vaccine was with a public-private partnership that committed government money to eliminate the financial risk for companies willing to expedite the research and production of a safe vaccine.

In the Rose Garden, on 15 May, the president announced Operation Warp Speed, which aimed to develop safe and effective COVID-19 vaccines that would be produced and distributed before the end of the year. Many scoffed, but President Trump never wavered. He kept himself fully informed of developments and slashed every possible bit of red tape that might stand in the way of success. History, we knew, was against us. No vaccine had ever been developed and produced that fast. But President Trump was as confident in private as he was in public, and this became our medical "Manhattan Project."

President Trump brought on a vaccine expert in Moncef Slaoui as his chief adviser and head of Operation Warp Speed, and appointed army General Gus Perna, the senior army logistician expert, as the chief operations officer for the effort. Operation Warp Speed had three core strategies to succeed. The first was to build a broad portfolio of vaccine candidates, so that we could progress even if one or two failed. The second was to offer unprecedented government support, both money and manpower, to help with clinical trials. Third, the government would pay for the manufacture of the vaccines *even before they were approved for use.* Vaccines would still have to go through rigorous clinical development and independent regulatory review and approval, but this way we would cut nine months to a year from the time line of vaccine development and distribution. It would save hundreds of thousands of lives.

The scientific process is exacting, as it should be, and though we pushed for speed, we did not cut corners on safety. In fact, when we needed to slow things down, briefly, to ensure we had the right demographics in the clinical trials, we did that—and no one pushed back.

What we all thought was outrageous was vice presidential candidate Kamala Harris's politicization of the vaccine, with her statement in October that "if the public health professionals, if Dr. Fauci, if the doctors tell us that we should take it, I'll be the first in line to take it—absolutely. But if Donald Trump tells us we should take it, I'm not taking it." She became the public face of the anti-vaccine movement. Her statement only illustrated the illogical, irrational, perverse obsession the Democrats had with hating Donald Trump, because the president could not, on his own authority, authorize a vaccine for use—and he had no incentive to do so. His incentive was to make the system work better and faster than it had ever worked before. He drove the vaccine development as much as any chief executive could, but we removed no safety guards; the actual vaccine was developed by doctors and scientists, not by Trump; and Kamala Harris's statement was nothing more than the most shameless political theater meant to push an counterfactual narrative of hate against the president. So much for confidence-building, so much for caring about the American people, so much for "following the science."

On 11 December 2020, the Food and Drug Administration's Dr. Stephen Hahn approved recommendations for emergency use authorization for the first COVID-19 vaccine, one made by Pfizer. America had succeeded through extensive clinical trials to produce a vaccine in under a year. In a stunning announcement, based on evidence from clinical trials, the Pfizer vaccine was 95 percent effective at preventing symptomatic infection. Moderna's vaccine would shortly follow with a similar efficacy rate. To give a comparison, effectiveness of the measles vaccine is 97 percent, the annual flu shot around 44 percent. Truly, there was now light at the end of the long tunnel of the pandemic. We all knew an effective vaccine, well distributed, would break the pandemic's grip on the world.

On Monday, 14 December, Vice President Pence had a teleconference with the nation's governors in which he said that "we are at the beginning of the end on Covid. Today is day one of that beginning." He told the gathering, "We cut red tape but cut no corners." General Perna informed the governors that vaccines had already been delivered to 145 sites and that almost three million doses would be delivered by the end of the week. Governor Jim Justice of West Virginia said, "You guys have done a helluva good job." Governor Greg Abbott of Texas said the speed of getting to a vaccine was "a miracle." Forty-five governors were on that call, and they had the same sense that we did: we were on the road to ending the pandemic. Even Alisyn Camerota, reporting for the liberal, Trump-hating CNN, said, on air, that the vaccine "timeline has been jaw-dropping."

After the teleconference, I walked into the vice president's office and shook his hand. I told him, "Sir, we need to get you vaccinated." The president had caught COVID-19; the First Lady had as well. Only two people on the vice president's team had not been hit: me and the vice president. (It did not make me feel any better when in the previous week our head of communications, Katie Miller, said to me, "I can't believe you haven't caught it.")

The vice president told me that he would not jump the queue; he would get vaccinated when it fell his turn, given his age and general good health. I pressed him and said that for "continuity of government" purposes it was important that he be vaccinated so that we wouldn't be without him for any period of time. I got "the look," which meant the discussion was over.

It was typical Mike Pence, wait till everyone else is taken care of. To me, it was a national security issue. President Trump had already had the virus, so he was protected; Pence wasn't. I called Gus Perna and told him we needed to ensure there were shots set for the national security team. Gus had me covered and said, "Vaccines are already at the White House."

Tuesday afternoon I went to White House chief of staff Mark Meadows and said I needed help in convincing the vice president to take the shot. I told Mark it would build confidence in the vaccine. The vaccine had already been trashed during the campaign by Joe Biden and Kamala Harris, and among the general public there was a noticeable reluctance to take it. Mark told me to go to the White House clinic and get vaccinated myself. "Your getting vaccinated will help me convince the vice president." I got the Pfizer vaccine that night and had no adverse reaction. The next morning, I went in early to see the vice president and said, "You and the Second Lady need to get vaccinated. It will only turn your hair white." I got the "look" again but that Friday he and the Second Lady took the shot in front of national cameras and said, "Help is on the way." He was right. On Inauguration Day alone, about 1.5 million vaccine shots were given.

We led the world in developing a vaccine and were leading the world in vaccinations. The vaccines would effectively end the pandemic. Warp Speed will go down in history as an unqualified success. President Trump drove it with his tenacity and Vice President Pence helped coordinate the entire effort. Someone will someday write the full and fair history of Operation Warp Speed, and I am convinced that history will be kind.

CHAPTER SIXTEEN

End Game

As I drove into the White House early on 6 January 2021, it felt like the beginning of the end. A joint session of Congress would certify the Electoral College vote from the contested presidential election. The vice president, as president of the Senate, would in turn certify the results from each state. It was, politically speaking, akin to watching your own funeral.

Coming down E Street and approaching the White House complex, massive crowds were already moving to the Ellipse for a major "Stop the Steal" rally, protesting the certification of an election when there were still concerns about voting irregularities. President Trump believed that massive voter fraud had denied him re-election. Some Republicans wanted a better accounting for the alleged irregularities. But it seemed as though even if fraud could be definitively proven on a scale large enough to have changed the election results—and it hadn't been yet—it was too late. It would take too long to unravel in the courts, and the courts would to be loath to overturn the tabulated results anyway, even if there were legitimate questions about them.

That didn't stop many of us from continuing to have such questions. We had felt confident in the closing days of the election, and the election night results seemed to vindicate that confidence. I had gone to bed on election night seeing that we were comfortably ahead in Pennsylvania and Michigan, and, because of that, I assumed we were likely to win. A well-respected journalist had even sent me a phone message early in the morning hours that President Trump's numbers were "looking surprisingly good."

But when I woke up, our 100,000-vote margins in both Pennsylvania and Michigan were gone because more recently tabulated ballots, in huge ballot drops, had gone to Biden by something like 90 percent margins. To me, it seemed statistically questionable. There were many explanations offered for these dramatic changes, but none, to many of us, seemed terribly convincing. At least, none were more convincing than the possibility that Democratic officials, in their frenzy to be rid of Trump, had gone beyond bending the rules governing voting (sometimes without the approval of their state legislatures) to taking advantage of the unprecedented use of more easily compromised mail-in ballots.

Three days later, news outlets declared Joe Biden the winner. The final vote numbers were stunning, with Trump getting eleven million more votes than he had in the 2016 election and increasing his votes in heavily Hispanic districts. For the first time in one hundred years, Zapata County, Texas, which is 95 percent Hispanic, voted for a Republican. Nationally, Trump bettered his 2016 performance with Hispanic voters and black voters, yet he strangely lost black voters by larger margins in Detroit, Milwaukee, and Philadelphia, which was why he lost Michigan, Wisconsin, and Pennsylvania. Of the nineteen so-called bellwether counties that have accurately predicted presidential outcomes since 1980, eighteen of them voted for Trump, including Valencia County, New Mexico, which had gone with the winning candidate in every presidential election since 1952. It wasn't just the bellwether counties where President Trump did well. According to pollster Patrick Basham, Biden "won a record low of 17 percent" of counties in the United States.

In a 5 January 2021 opinion piece for *The Hill*, political consultant and columnist John Feehery wrote, "I don't know if there was enough provable fraud in this last election to swing the election back to Trump. But to say that this election was purer than the driven snow is not defensible either." Lance Morrow, writing in the *Wall Street Journal* on 4 April 2020, reflected on the tightness of the outcome by writing, "Leave aside Donald Trump's claims that the election was stolen; it was, without argument, close. The result would seem to call not for a radical transformation of the country but, rather, for compromise, reconciliation and the retraction of ideological claws." The *Los Angeles Times* noted in December 2020 that "Biden won by just a little more than 43,000 votes—the combined margins in Arizona, Georgia and Wisconsin, his three closest states. Flip just those three to red [to Trump], and the electoral college would have landed in a 269–269 tie, sending the contest to the House of Representatives, a likely Trump victory and a true constitutional crisis." Interestingly, the Republican Party gained fourteen congressional seats in the 2020 election. In a rare turn of events, the president's party gained House seats and did well in state elections, while he lost the White House. Suffice it to say, there were serious, legitimate questions about the integrity of the election. The margin of votes that could have changed the outcome was relatively small, and the president, to say the least, was not a quitter, even when the odds against him were high. Many of his voters felt cheated by the result and frustrated that their questions weren't being answered. The crowd forming for the 6 January rally was resolute, but they were not an angry mob. I had been to a lot of Trump rallies over the previous five years. People were always enthused and happy, festive and upbeat. The crowds were never mad or violent or destructive. This crowd seemed no different. The people I saw moving down 17th Street were not menacing. The Secret Service certainly expected no trouble. They were not in riot gear and there was no extra security around the White House or the Capitol.

The president had thrown every legal challenge he had at the election results and had come up empty. We had been running against the clock, and today, the clock would run out. I thought of the rally as a last hurrah.

That morning, I briefed the president on national security issues, chiefly our progress in Afghanistan. But the upcoming votes in Congress were clearly on his mind. He was scheduled to address the rally at 10:30 a.m. but in fact would not start speaking until around 11:50. By the time he finished addressing the crowd, the House and Senate would be in joint session with Vice President Pence presiding. I expected the president's remarks at the rally to be strong, yet measured.

Before leaving the White House, Trump called Pence, asking him to return the electoral votes of several states to their respective state legislatures to be recertified. The president believed that given the opportunity, several state legislatures, reviewing alleged voting irregularities, might alter their states' Electoral College votes. The vice president was as concerned about voting irregularities as the rest of us, but believed that this was not his constitutional role, and he refused the president's request. What would be allowed would be a two-hour debate on formal and specific objections raised by members of Congress. Once the objections were resolved, the House and Senate would then vote to accept or reject the Electoral College results.

After the call, I joined the presidential motorcade to the Ellipse. The rally was massive, reaching from the Ellipse to the Washington Monument and beyond. I would guess there were easily 150,000 people there.

The president spoke for an hour. His frustration was clear, as was his determination: "We will never give up; we will never concede."

The president encouraged the crowd, saying, "If Mike Pence does the right thing, we win the election....States want to revote. The states got defrauded. They were given false information. They voted on it. Now they want to recertify. They want it back....I know that everyone here will soon be marching over to the Capitol building to peacefully and patriotically make your voices heard. Today we will see whether Republicans stand strong for integrity of our elections."

Before Trump had even finished his remarks, there was conflict at the Capitol. In that apparently peaceful crowd were scattered groups of troublemakers, and the Capitol Police were clearly not prepared for the number of angry protesters; nor had they had any reason to expect violence or a riot, given the experience of previous Trump rallies. The

Capitol Police were overwhelmed. Anyone who knows a thing about riot control will tell you, once the mass of a mob is moving and it breaches the first line of "defense," you are best served by letting the riot run its course, and run out of steam, while you revert to "point defense" of critical areas or people. This is especially true when the rioters, like those who attacked the Capitol, are not well armed, are not burning things, and appear more interested in trespassing than in fighting.

By this time, I was back in the White House, watching the television feeds. Initial surprise gave way to an immediate discussion of how to respond to the mobbing of the Capitol. White House chief of staff Mark Meadows wanted to know when we could expect National Guard support. It was coming, but slowly.

On 3 January, the president had asked the Defense Department to deploy National Guard troops to protect the rally. He was worried that counter-protesters might attempt to subvert his supporters' peaceful right of assembly. The Defense Department, however, was worried about the "optics" of a large deployment of National Guard troops, so instead it had a "quick reaction force" twelve miles away that could be called upon in case of an emergency. Well, now we had our emergency—and the troops were too far away for a rapid response.

At 2:38 p.m., 6 January, the president, who had praised the Secret Service and law enforcement in his remarks at the rally, tweeted, "Please support our Capitol Police and Law Enforcement. They are truly on the side of our Country. Stay peaceful."

But it was too late. Capitol security had been breached by rioters.

The House and Senate chambers were evacuated. The vice president was taken to a secure area. With the help of the U.S. Secret Service operations center, I kept President Trump informed of our security measures, including the vice president's location and safety.

It was a raw and terrible day for everyone. Later in the evening, after order was restored, the vote to certify the Electoral College results continued. The only immediate effect of the riot was to discourage and discredit any further objections to the Electoral College results. Joe

Biden was officially declared the Electoral College winner at 3:41 a.m. Trump tweeted, "There will be an orderly transition on January 20."

A vindictive Congress attempted to impeach and convict the president yet again, this time for the events of 6 January, and even after he became a private citizen. The effort failed—and rightly so. I was in President Trump's proximity that entire day. I can say categorically that he never intended there to be violence, that he did not attempt to incite violence, and that none of us, given our previous experience at Trump rallies, ever envisioned that a riot would follow the president's remarks. The president was playing his last—and legitimate—constitutional card. The president was true to form, a fighter to the end. But the idea that a crowd that became a mob that broke into the Capitol and then wandered around the halls amounted to an "insurrection" was ludicrous. It was a mob gone bad, but an insurrection it was not. That the charge was leveled by many of the very same people who had encouraged violent leftist riots throughout the summer and beyond was worse than cynical and hypocritical. It was an unfortunate end to our administration, but also an unhappy warning about what would follow: a new administration that would allow an objectively radical, leftist agenda and immediately seek to obliterate nearly everything we had achieved. We had 1,461 days in the White House. Of those, 1,460 were pretty good. President Trump achieved a lot for America.

What were those achievements? Well, for starters:

- We defeated the largest terrorist caliphate in the world, ISIS.
- We killed its terrorist leader, Abu Bakr al-Baghdadi.
- We eliminated the foremost terrorist in the world, Qasem Soleimani.
- We wound down the Afghan War and passed the new administration a workable plan to finally end America's longest war.

- Through the Abraham Accords, we greatly improved the prospects for peace in the Middle East, lessened Arab-Israeli tensions, and organized a de facto Arab-Israeli alliance against Iran.
- In support of Israel we directed the move of our embassy from Tel Aviv to Jerusalem twenty-three years after passage of the Jerusalem Embassy Act of 1995.
- We built up our military, increased defense budgets and readiness, and funded the modernization of our entire nuclear triad.
- We pushed and prodded our NATO allies to do more for their own defense as agreed in the 2014 Wales Declaration.
- We challenged China economically and politically.
- We held the first U.S.–North Korea summit and greatly lowered military tensions in the Korean peninsula.
- We withdrew from the flawed "Iran deal," which, as negotiated, allowed for the expiration of all sanctions and restrictions on Iran while not allowing for unrestricted inspections and other measures to prevent Iran from developing nuclear weapons.
- We created a new Space Force and revitalized NASA. We sent NASA astronauts into space from American soil for the first time in nine years.
- We came to diplomatic agreements with Mexico and the Northern Triangle countries (El Salvador, Guatemala, and Honduras) that strengthened our southern border and greatly curtailed illegal immigration.
- The president appointed more than 230 "originalist" judges to the federal courts, and three justices to the Supreme Court, who see their role as upholding the original intent of the Constitution, defending our civil

and religious liberties, and not legislating from the bench.

- We replaced old and unfair trade deals, like NAFTA, with new and better ones, like USMCA, that put American interests first.
- We encouraged and achieved American energy independence. In 2019, the United States became a net exporter of all oil products.
- The president's economic agenda, including tax cuts and slashed regulatory red tape, gave our country its strongest economy since World War II, with record low unemployment—until we were hit by the pandemic.
- To respond to the pandemic, we initiated a public-private partnership, Operation Warp Speed, that delivered three new vaccines to the American people in record time, a historic achievement. We developed an effective vaccine distribution plan that was delivering more than one million vaccinations a day before Inauguration Day.
- He signed the Tax Cuts and Jobs Act of 2017, which significantly reduced tax rates for businesses and individuals and increased the standard family deduction and family tax credits. The economy boomed.

These are all facts, there in black and white. They were achieved through political infighting—against a hostile, even hysterical press, an opposition party that deemed itself "the resistance," a Republican establishment that was, at best, lukewarm in its support for the president, and current or former Republican "never-Trumpers" who vociferously opposed the president. For four years, it seemed as if we were under constant political siege. President Trump never enjoyed a post-election "honeymoon" in Washington. There were calls for his impeachment even before his inauguration.

■ ■ ■

The extremism of the reaction against Trump became even more worrying to me when I recognized that it was part of a bigger picture, a culture war against our past, against traditional American heroes, against American patriotism and conservatism in the broadest possible sense, in the sense of conserving our culture and in the sense of honoring and learning from our history.

During the summer 2020 riots, as cities were set on fire, law enforcement and federal buildings attacked, and businesses looted and vandalized, statues of American heroes—from Christopher Columbus to Ulysses S. Grant, from Benjamin Franklin to Abraham Lincoln, from Thomas Jefferson to Andrew Jackson—were defaced or toppled, or simply packed away and removed by state and local governments and colleges and universities. Schools named after American presidents or the Founding Fathers were renamed. It was a bonfire of destruction of American history, an overt attempt to desecrate and obliterate our shared past.

The president thought it was wrong, and so did I.

The last National Defense Authorization Act that came across his desk included the creation of a commission to consider renaming military posts, roads, and buildings named after Confederate leaders. In early December, we discussed the issue in the Oval Office. In the room were Vice President Pence, Secretary of Defense Mark Esper, and chairman of the Joint Chiefs General Mark Milley. I sat where I normally did, near the rear of the room, where I knew I could always catch the president's eye.

Fort Bragg, where I had spent much of my military career, was named after Confederate general Braxton Bragg. Fort Benning, where I had trained, was named after Confederate general Henry L. Benning. I had lived at Fort Myer, where there is Lee Avenue, named after Confederate general Robert E. Lee. Not only am I an avid student of American history, but I had lived and trained and worked where America's "mystic

chords of memory," as Lincoln put it, were respected. I knew why these
men had been recognized. In their lives, they had fought for the United
States and for the Confederacy. I knew that these names stood for the
reunification and reconciliation of our country after a bitter civil war of
state against state, brother against brother. Perhaps no one had said it
better than Theodore Roosevelt:

> The great Civil War, in which Lincoln towered as the loftiest
> figure, left us not only a reunited country, but a country that
> has the proud right to claim as its own the glory won alike by
> those who wore the blue and by those who wore the gray, by
> those who followed Ulysses Grant and by those who followed
> Robert E. Lee, for both fought with equal bravery and equal
> sincerity of conviction, each striving for the light as it was
> given him to see the light; though it is now clear to all that the
> triumph of the cause of freedom and of the Union was essen-
> tial to the welfare of mankind.

The Oval Office discussion soon turned to Robert E. Lee, as he, more
than anyone else, more even than Confederate president Jefferson Davis,
represented the South in our memory of the Civil War. Lee also represented the poignant choice that had faced many Southern-born officers.
Just before the war, at the Blair House across the street from the White
House, Lee had been offered command of the Union Army. He turned
it down because, while he had opposed secession, he would not consent
to fight his own native state, and vowed that save in defense of Virginia,
he would not fight at all.

President Trump asked General Milley and Secretary Esper what
they thought. They said they had no problem with the renaming commission, because "Lee was a traitor."

I caught the president's eye and he asked me, "General, what do you
think?"

I said that once you start, or endorse, this sort of cancel culture, it will not end with Confederate monuments or names, and no one will be able to control it. We had seen that already. But more than that, I opposed going after Confederate leaders because it was a denial of an important part of American history.

I pointed to the White House residence and reminded everyone in the room that in June 1865, President Andrew Johnson had met there with General Ulysses S. Grant. Johnson had wanted Lee court-martialed. Ulysses S. Grant told him: if you do that, you find yourself a new general.

I looked at Esper and Milley and said, "We need to learn from history, not destroy it. What would you do with the Confederate Monument in Arlington National Cemetery, with hundreds of Confederate graves around it? That monument was supported by William Howard Taft when he was secretary of war and later as president. It's a memorial that President Obama honored in 2009, when he sent a wreath on Confederate Memorial Day." I was on a roll. "Our nation has a complex history," I said. "It should be studied, not cancelled. If we support this renaming commission, we are contributing to the cancellation of American history." I let my eyes flit between General Milley and Secretary Esper and concluded: "Neither of you is a Ulysses S. Grant."

There was a short pause and then the president asked me, "Where are you from?"

I'm sure, despite all our time together, he assumed I was from the South. I said, "Mr. President, I am from California, but I love this nation, warts and all. Killing history means we are killing a bit of ourselves."

I strongly believe that—and I was saddened that so many Republicans in Congress joined with Democrats in denying it. If only one side fights this culture war, then only one side can win it, and I think it's the wrong side. That, ultimately, is the battle before us now, a battle for the soul of this nation, for defining what America is, was, and shall be. We are a great nation. All great nations have troubled periods, but we have learned from ours. Canceling parts of our history kills part of our nation's soul. It is wrong.

I'm staying in the fight. I'm used to conflict. I have been in many battles and fought in many wars. I've witnessed death and come too close to it far too often. I've made tough calls and hard decisions. In truth, I have spent nearly my entire life preparing for confrontations, the big and the small. In some ways, I was uniquely prepared for working in the Trump White House, and I have no regrets about my time with President Trump and Vice President Pence; it was all worth the fight. Yet the war for America's future is obviously not won. President Biden ran as a unifier, but we are now more fractured than ever before. I was fortunate to serve a president who believed in America and Americans first. A president who did not take a paycheck but donated his salary to charities or to agencies helping Americans. A leader who was focused first on our citizens, not people from somewhere else. A public brawler, but one with extreme compassion behind closed doors. The perfect leader for America First. The fight goes on. I believe the hardest battles are yet in front of us, and I, for one, am ready.

Acknowledgments

I want to begin by thanking the most important people that I have been privileged to serve through my life—you, the American people. I love this nation and her people, and I have been honored to serve.

A great thank you to Stuart Epperson, who took a chance on this book when others bowed out, and the whole Regnery team, who have been so supportive. Especially Tom Spence, Harry Crocker, and Kathleen Curran, who guided me through the process.

To the soldiers, non-commissioned officers and officers from the 101st Airborne, Special Forces, 7th Infantry (Light), 82nd Airborne. I have been so honored to serve with you. To those I could not bring back from battle, you are always in my thoughts and prayers. I pray we will meet again.

To my Mom and Dad and my brothers, Mike and Jeff, and sister, Kathie, for all the years we have spent together. Mom and Dad raised us right with love and respect that continue to this day.

There were those I called when challenging missions were given and for that, Jim Jackson, Bert Ges, and Steve England will always be in my memory. Thanks for moving to the sounds of guns with me when I asked.

The drive for me to write this book was our forty-fifth president, Donald J. Trump, whom I was fortunate to serve alongside as a candidate and president. Every day was interesting, and behind closed doors I saw the goodness in his heart for wanting what was right for America.

Along this journey I have been blessed by my family, who have been the anchor for my life. My wife Paige and three wonderful children, Bryan, Meaghan, and Tyler. Our family is lucky to include our son-in-law, Mike, and daughter-in-law, Gemma. Our grandchildren, Pepper, Madison, Alex, and Luke—this fight has been for you. I love you all so very much.

And to you, the readers, I hope you felt the joy of the journey. I pray I served you well.

Index